THE BAIT OF SATAN

JOHN BEVERE

CHARISMA
HOUSE

Most CHARISMA HOUSE BOOK GROUP products are available at special quantity discounts for bulk purchase for sales promotions, premiums, fund-raising, and educational needs. For details, write Charisma House Book Group, 600 Rinehart Road, Lake Mary, Florida 32746, or telephone (407) 333-0600.

THE BAIT OF SATAN by John Bevere
Published by Charisma House
Charisma Media/Charisma House Book Group
600 Rinehart Road
Lake Mary, Florida 32746
www.charismahouse.com

Unless otherwise noted, all Scripture quotations are from the New King James Version of the Bible. Copyright © 1979, 1980, 1982 by Thomas Nelson, Inc., publishers. Used by permission.

Scripture quotations marked KJV are from the King James Version of the Bible.

Scripture quotations marked NIV are from the Holy Bible, New International Version. Copyright © 1973, 1978, 1984, International Bible Society. Used by permission.

Cover design by Justin Evans

Copyright © 1994, 1997, 2004, 2011 by John Bevere
All rights reserved

First edition, 1994, 1997
Revised edition, 2004

The Library of Congress has catalogued the previous edition as follows:

Bevere, John.
The bait of Satan / John Bevere.-- Rev. ed.
    p. cm.
    Includes bibliographical references.
    ISBN 1-59185-413-X (pbk.)
    1. Forgiveness--Religious aspects--Christianity. 2. Interpersonal
        conflict--Religious aspects--Christianity. I. Title.
    BV4647.F55B48 2004
    234'.5--dc22
                                        2004003796

International Standard Book Number: 978-1-61638-196-7
E-book ISBN: 978-1-59979-304-7

19 20 21 22 23 — 18 17 16 15 14
Printed in the United States of America

MY DEEPEST
APPRECIATION TO...

My wife, Lisa, who, next to the Lord, is my most cherished friend. You are truly a virtuous woman. I will be forever grateful to the Lord for joining us as man and wife. Thank you for selflessly helping with the editing of this book.

To my four sons, Addison, Austin, Alexander, and Arden, who sacrificed time with Daddy so this project could be completed. You boys are a joy to my heart.

A special thanks to John Mason, who believed in this message and encouraged me to pursue publishing it; to Deborah Poulalion, for her talents and support in editing; and to the entire Charisma House staff who labored with us in this project.

Most important, my sincere gratitude to our Father in heaven for His indescribable gift; to our Lord Jesus for His grace, truth, and love; and to the Holy Spirit for His faithful guidance during this project.

CONTENTS

PREFACE

THE BOOK YOU HOLD IS QUITE POSSIBLY THE MOST IMPORTANT confrontation with truth you'll encounter in your lifetime. I can say this with confidence, not because I've written it, but because of its subject matter. The issue of offense—the very core of *The Bait of Satan*—is often the most difficult obstacle an individual must face and overcome.

The disciples of Jesus witnessed many great and notable miracles. They watched in amazement as blind eyes were opened and the dead were raised. They heard Jesus command a life-threatening storm to stillness. They saw thousands fed by the miracle of multiplication of a few loaves and fish. The list of Jesus's miracles and wonders was so inexhaustible that, according to the Bible, the world of books could not contain it.

Never before had mankind witnessed the miraculous hand of God in such an overwhelming and tangible way. Amazed and awed as the disciples were, it was not these miracles that pushed them to the brink of doubt. No, that challenge would come later toward the end of Jesus's earthly ministry. Jesus had instructed His disciples, "If your brother sins against you...seven times in a day, and seven times in a day returns to you, saying, 'I repent,' you shall forgive him." Their immediate response to Him was, "Increase our faith" (Luke 17:3–5). The miracles had not inspired a cry for greater faith, or for the raising of the dead, or for a calmed sea; but the simple command to forgive those who have wronged you!

Jesus said, "It is impossible that no offenses should come" (Luke 17:1). It is not a question of opportunity to be offended, but what your response will be. It is an unfortunate fact that, not some, but many are offended and held captive.

It has been more than fifteen years since this book was launched. In this time period we've received countless letters and numerous testimonies of individual lives, families, and ministries that have been healed and transformed by the truths from the Word of God contained in this book. We have included a sampling for your encouragement. For all of them, we rejoice and give God all the glory!

One leader shared, "Our church was in the middle of a huge split. It looked hopeless. I gave a copy of *The Bait of Satan* to every elder. The split was diverted, and we are one today!"

Many marriages have been saved. Recently after speaking in Nebraska, a couple approached me. The wife confessed, "I was offended ten years ago by the leaders in this church. I became bitter and suspicious, constantly defending myself and my position. My marriage suffered from my anguish, and my husband was in the process of divorcing me. He was unsaved and wanted nothing to do with the church. Someone put a copy of *The Bait of Satan* in my hands. I read it and, within a short time, was completely set free from offense and bitterness. When my husband saw the changes in my life, he surrendered his life to the lordship of Jesus Christ and stopped the divorce proceedings." The husband stood by his wife, smiling. When she had finished sharing, he affirmed the wonderful changes in his life and home!

The testimony that touched my heart the most occurred when I ministered in Naples, Florida. Just before I spoke, a burly, middle-aged man stood up before the congregation and wept as he relayed his tragic story: "All my life I have felt like there was a wall between me and God. I would attend meetings where others sensed God's presence, while I watched detached and numb. Even when I prayed there was no release or presence. Several weeks ago I was handed the book *The Bait of Satan*. I read it in its entirety. I realized I had taken Satan's bait years ago. I hated my mother for abandoning me when I was six months old. I realized I had to go to her and forgive. I called and spoke with her for only the second time in thirty-six years. I cried, 'Mom, I have held unforgiveness toward you all my life for giving me away.' She began to weep and said, 'Son, I have hated myself for the last thirty-six years for leaving you.'"

He continued, "I forgave her, and she forgave herself; now we are reconciled."

Then came the exciting part. "Now the wall that separated me from God's presence is gone!"

At this point, he just completely lost it and wept. He struggled to get these last words out, "Now I cry in the presence of God like a baby."

I know the strength and reality of that captivity. I had been held hostage to its numb torment for years. This book is not a theory; it is God's Word made flesh. It brims with truths I have personally walked through. I believe it will strengthen you. As you read, ask the Master to increase your faith! As you grow in faith, He will receive glory and you shall be filled with joy! May God richly bless you.

—JOHN BEVERE

INTRODUCTION

ANYONE WHO HAS TRAPPED ANIMALS KNOWS A TRAP NEEDS ONE of two things to be successful. It must be hidden, in the hope that an animal will stumble upon it, and it must be baited to lure the animal into the trap's deadly jaws.

Satan, the enemy of our souls, incorporates both of these strategies as he lays out his most deceptive and deadly traps. They are both hidden and baited.

Satan, along with his cohorts, is not as blatant as many believe. He is subtle and delights in deception. He is shrewd in his operations...cunning and crafty. Don't forget he can disguise himself as a messenger of light. If we are not trained by the Word of God to divide rightly between good and evil, we won't recognize his traps for what they are.

One of his most deceptive and insidious kinds of bait is something every Christian has encountered—offense. Actually, offense itself is not deadly—if it stays in the trap. But if we pick it up and consume it and feed on it in our hearts, then we have become offended. Offended people produce much fruit, such as hurt, anger, outrage, jealousy, resentment, strife, bitterness, hatred, and envy. Some of the consequences of picking up an offense are insults, attacks, wounding, division, separation, broken relationships, betrayal, and backsliding.

Often those who are offended do not even realize they are trapped. They are oblivious to their condition because they are so focused on the wrong that was done to them. They are in denial. The most effective way for the enemy to blind us is to cause us to focus on ourselves.

This book exposes this deadly trap and reveals how to escape its grip and stay free from it. Freedom from offense is essential for every

1

Christian because Jesus said it is impossible to live this life and not have the opportunity to be offended (Luke 17:1).

In churches across America and in other nations where I have preached this message, over 50 percent of the people have responded to the altar call. Although this is a high response, it still is not everyone. Pride holds some people back from responding. I have seen people healed, set free, filled with the Holy Spirit, and receive answers to prayers when they are released from this trap. They usually report that they have sought for years what they received in a moment, once they were free.

In the last part of the twentieth century, knowledge has greatly increased in the church. But even with this increase it seems we have experienced more division among believers, leaders, and congregations. The reason: Offense is rampant from a lack of genuine love. "Knowledge puffs up, but love edifies" (1 Cor. 8:1). So many are snared in this deceptive trap that we have almost come to believe it is a normal way of life.

Before the return of Christ, however, true believers will be united unlike anything in the past. I believe that today countless men and women will be released from this trap of offense. This will be one of the main links in seeing revival sweep this nation. Unbelievers will behold Jesus through our love of one another where they had been blinded to Him before.

I do not believe in writing a book just to write one. God has burned this message into my heart, and I have seen its fruit remain. One pastor said to me after a service in which this message was preached, "I have never seen so many set free at one time."

God has spoken to my heart that this is only the beginning. Many will be set free, healed, and restored as they read this book and obey the Spirit's prompting to them. I am believing as you read the words on these pages that the Teacher and Counselor will apply them personally to you. As He does, this revealed word will bring a great liberty to your life and ministry.

Let's pray together as you begin:

Father, in the name of Jesus, I ask that You would reveal, by Your Spirit, Your Word to me as I read this book. Expose any hidden areas of my heart that have hindered me from knowing

You and serving You more effectively. I welcome the conviction of Your Spirit and ask for Your grace to carry out what You desire of me. May I come to know You more intimately as a result of hearing Your voice through reading this book.

OUR RESPONSE
TO AN OFFENSE DETERMINES
OUR FUTURE.

The Bait of Satan has changed our lives and our ministry. We have watched the video at least twenty times and read the book over and over. Our ministry has used the book and video teachings to transform our lives as well as the lives of many others. The message is powerful and timely.

CHAPTER 1

ME, OFFENDED?

It is impossible that no offenses should come.
—LUKE 17:1

A S I TRAVEL ACROSS THE UNITED STATES MINISTERING, I HAVE been able to observe one of the enemy's most deadly and deceptive traps. It imprisons countless Christians, severs relationships, and widens the existing breaches between us. It is the trap of offense.

Many are unable to function properly in their calling because of the wounds and hurts that offenses have caused in their lives. They are handicapped and hindered from fulfilling their full potential. Most often it is a fellow believer who has hurt them. This causes the offense to feel like a betrayal. In Psalm 55:12–14 David laments, "For it is not an enemy who reproaches me; then I could bear it. Nor is it one who hates me who has exalted himself against me; then I could hide from him. But it was you, a man my equal, my companion and my acquaintance. We took sweet counsel together, and walked to the house of God in the throng."

They are those whom we sit with and sing alongside, or perhaps it is the one who is delivering the sermon. We spend holidays, attend social functions, and share offices with them. Or perhaps it is closer. We grow up with, confide in, and sleep next to them. The closer the relationship, the more severe the offense! You find the greatest hatred among people who were once close.

Attorneys will tell you the most vicious cases are in the divorce courts. The American media constantly report murders in homes by desperate family members. The home, meant to be a shelter of protection, provision, and growth where we learn to give and receive love, is often the very root of our pain. History shows that the bloodiest wars are civil—brother against brother, son against father, or father against son.

The possibilities for offense are as endless as the list of relationships, no matter how complex or simple. This truth remains: Only those you care about can hurt you. You expect more from them—after all, you've given more of yourself to them. The higher the expectations, the greater the fall.

Selfishness reigns in our society. Men and women today look out for themselves to the neglect and hurt of those around them. This should not surprise us. The Bible is very clear that in the last days men will be "lovers of themselves" (2 Tim. 3:2). We expect this in unbelievers, but Paul was not referring to those outside the church. He was talking about those within it. Many are wounded, hurt, and bitter. They are offended! But they do not realize that they have fallen into Satan's trap.

Is it our fault? Jesus made it very clear that it is impossible to live in this world and not have the opportunity to become offended. Yet most believers are shocked, bewildered, and amazed when it happens. We believe we are the only ones who have been wronged. This response leaves us vulnerable to a root of bitterness. Therefore we must be prepared and armed for offenses, because our response determines our future.

THE DECEPTIVE TRAP

The Greek word for "offend" in Luke 17:1 comes from the word *skandalon*. This word originally referred to the part of the trap to which the bait was attached. Hence the word signifies laying a trap in someone's way.[1] In the New Testament it often describes an entrapment used by the enemy. Offense is a tool of the devil to bring people into captivity. Paul instructed young Timothy:

And a servant of the Lord must not quarrel but be gentle to all, able to teach, patient, in humility correcting those *who are in opposition,* if God perhaps will grant them repentance, so that they may know the truth, and that they may come to their senses and *escape the snare [entrapment] of the devil,* having been *taken captive by him to do his will.*

—2 TIMOTHY 2:24–26, EMPHASIS ADDED

Those who are in quarrels or opposition fall into a trap and are held prisoner to do the devil's will. Even more alarming, they are unaware of their captivity! Like the prodigal they must come to themselves by awaking to their true condition. They do not realize that they are spewing out bitter waters rather than pure. When a person is deceived, he believes he is right even though he is not.

No matter what the scenario is, we can divide all offended people into two major categories: (1) those who have been treated unjustly and (2) those who *believe* they have been treated unjustly. People in the second category believe with all their hearts that they have been wronged. Often their conclusions are drawn from inaccurate information. Or their information is accurate, but their conclusion is distorted. Either way, they hurt, and their understanding is darkened. They judge by assumption, appearance, and hearsay.

THE HEART'S TRUE CONDITION

One way the enemy keeps a person in an offended state is to keep the offense hidden, cloaked with pride. Pride will keep you from admitting your true condition.

Once I was severely hurt by a couple of ministers. People would say, "I can't believe they did this to you. Aren't you hurt?"

I would quickly respond, "No, I am fine. I'm not hurt." I knew it was wrong to be offended, so I denied and repressed it. I convinced myself I was not, but in reality I was. Pride masked the true condition of my heart.

Pride keeps you from dealing with truth. It distorts your vision. You never change when you think everything is fine. Pride hardens your heart and dims the eyes of your understanding. It keeps you from the change of heart—repentance—that will set you free. (See 2 Timothy 2:24–26.)

Pride causes you to view yourself as a victim. Your attitude becomes, "I was mistreated and misjudged; therefore, I am justified in my behavior." Because you believe you are innocent and falsely accused, you hold back forgiveness. Though your true heart condition is hidden from you, it is *not* hidden from God. Just because you were mistreated, you do not have permission to hold on to an offense. Two wrongs do not make a right!

THE CURE

In the Book of Revelation Jesus addressed the church of Laodicea by first telling them how they saw themselves as rich, wealthy, and having need of nothing, then by exposing their true condition—"wretched, miserable, poor, blind, and naked" (Rev. 3:14–20). They had mistaken their financial strength for spiritual strength. Pride hid their true condition.

Many are this way today. They do not see the true condition of their hearts just as I was unable to see the resentment I carried toward those ministers. I had convinced myself I was not hurt. Jesus told the Laodiceans how to get out of their deception: buy God's gold and see their true condition.

Buy God's gold.

Jesus' first instruction for breaking free from deception was to "buy from Me gold refined in the fire" (Rev. 3:18).

Refined gold is soft and pliable, free from corrosion or other substances. It is when gold is mixed with other metals (copper, iron, nickel, and so on) that it becomes hard, less pliable, and more corrosive. This mixture is called an alloy. The higher the percentage of foreign metals, the harder the gold becomes. Conversely, the lower the percentage of alloy, the softer and more flexible the gold is.

Immediately we see the parallel: A pure heart is like pure gold—soft, tender, and pliable. Hebrews 3:13 states that hearts are hardened through the deceitfulness of sin! If we do not deal with an offense, it will produce more fruit of sin, such as bitterness, anger, and resentment. This added substance hardens our hearts just as alloys harden gold. This reduces or removes tenderness, creating a loss of sensitivity. We are hindered in our ability to hear God's voice. Our accuracy to see is darkened. This is a perfect setting for deception.

The first step in refining gold is grinding it into a powder and mixing it with a substance called flux. Then the mixture is placed in a furnace and melted by intense heat. The alloys and impurities are drawn to the flux and rise to the surface. The gold (which is heavier) remains at the bottom. The impurities or *dross* (such as copper, iron, and zinc, combined with flux) is then removed, yielding a purer metal.

Now look at what God says:

> Behold, I have refined you, but not as silver; I have tested you in the furnace of affliction.
>
> —Isaiah 48:10

And again:

> In this you greatly rejoice, though now for a little while, if need be, you have been grieved by *various trials,* that the genuineness of your faith, being much more precious than gold that perishes, though *it is tested by fire,* may be found to praise, honor, and glory at the revelation of Jesus Christ.
>
> —1 Peter 1:6–7, emphasis added

God refines with afflictions, trials, and tribulations, the heat of which separates impurities such as unforgiveness, strife, bitterness, anger, envy, and so forth from the character of God in our lives.

Sin easily hides where there is no heat of trials and afflictions. In times of prosperity and success, even a wicked man will seem kind and generous. Under the heat of trials, however, the impurities surface.

There was a time in my life when I went through intense trials such as I had never faced before. I became rude and harsh with those closest to me. My family and friends began to avoid me.

I cried out to the Lord, "Where is all this anger coming from? It wasn't here before!"

The Lord responded, "Son, it is when they liquefy gold in fire that the impurities show up." He then asked a question that changed my life. "Can you *see* the impurities in gold before it is put in the fire?"

"No," I answered.

"But that doesn't mean they were not there," He said. "When the fire of trials hit you, these impurities surfaced. Though hidden to you, they were always visible to Me. So now you have a choice that will determine your future. You can remain angry, blaming your wife, friends, pastor, and the people you work with, or you can see this dross of sin for what it is and repent, receive forgiveness, and I will take My ladle and remove these impurities from your life."

See your true condition.

Jesus said our ability to see correctly is another key to being freed from deception. Often when we are offended we see ourselves as victims and blame those who have hurt us. We justify our bitterness, unforgiveness, anger, envy, and resentment as they surface. Sometimes we even resent those who *remind* us of others who have hurt us. For this reason Jesus counseled, "Anoint your eyes with eye salve, that you may see" (Rev. 3:18). See what? Your true condition! That's the only way we can "be zealous and repent" as Jesus commanded next. You will only repent when you stop blaming other people.

When we blame others and defend our own position, we are blind. We struggle to remove the speck out of our brother's eye while there is a log in ours. It is the revelation of truth that brings freedom to us. When the Spirit of God shows us our sin, He always does it in such a way that it seems separate from us. This brings conviction, not condemnation.

It is my prayer that as you read this book, God's Word will enlighten the eyes of your understanding that you will see your true condition and become free from any offense you are harboring. Don't let pride keep you from seeing and repenting.

AN OFFENDED CHRISTIAN IS ONE WHO TAKES IN LIFE BUT, BECAUSE OF FEAR, CANNOT RELEASE IT.

Ten years ago, after twenty years of marriage, my husband walked out because he "was no longer happy." I was totally devastated. It has been a long time trying to get over the hurt, abandonment, and rejection his leaving caused. I asked God to help me to forgive him, and I truly thought I had, but I still carried hurt in my heart I could not get over. It was very painful whenever I had to see him. After reading *The Bait of Satan*, the Holy Spirit impressed me to speak to my ex-husband and ask him to forgive me for holding this offense. We talked for the first time in ten years. I truly believe I was healed and *set free!* I thank God for freeing me from this yoke of bondage that has enslaved me for so long.

—D. B., NEW YORK

CHAPTER 2

MASSIVE OFFENSE

And then many will be offended, will betray one another, and will hate one another. Then many false prophets will rise up and deceive many. And because lawlessness will abound, the love of many will grow cold. But he who endures to the end shall be saved.
—MATTHEW 24:10–13

IN THIS CHAPTER OF MATTHEW, JESUS IS GIVING THE SIGNS OF the end of this age. His disciples asked, "What will be the sign of Your coming?"

Most agree we are in the season of His return. It is useless to try to pinpoint the actual day of His return. Only the Father knows that. But Jesus said we would know *the season,* and it is now! Never before have we seen such prophetic fulfillment in the church, in Israel, and in nature. So we can confidently say that we are in the time period Jesus described in Matthew 24.

Notice one of the signs of His pending return: *"Many* will be offended...." Not a few, not some, but *many.*

First we must ask, "Who are these offended?" Are they Christians or just society in general? We find the answer as we continue to read: "And because lawlessness will abound, the *love* of many will grow cold." The Greek word for *love* in this verse is *agape.* There are several Greek words for *love* in the New Testament, but the two most common are *agape* and *phileo*.

Phileo defines a love found among friends. It is an affectionate love that is conditional. *Phileo* says, "You scratch my back, and I'll scratch yours," or "You treat me kindly, and I'll do the same."

On the other hand, *agape* is the love God sheds abroad in the hearts of His children. It is the same love Jesus gives freely to us. It is unconditional. It is not based on performance or even whether it is returned. It is a love that gives even when rejected.

Without God we can only love with a selfish love—one that cannot be given if it is not received and returned. However, *agape* loves regardless of the response. This *agape* is the love Jesus shed when He forgave from the cross. So "the many" Jesus refers to are Christians whose *agape* has grown cold.

There was a time when I did everything I could to show my love to a certain person. But it seemed that every time I reached out to love, the person slapped me back with criticism and harsh treatment. This went on for months. One day I was fed up.

I complained to God. "I have had it. Now You are going to have to talk to me about this. Every time I show Your love to this person, I get anger thrown back in my face!"

The Lord began to speak to me. "John, you need to develop faith in the love of God!"

"What do You mean?" I asked.

"He who sows to his flesh will of the flesh reap corruption," He explained, "but he who sows to the Spirit will of the Spirit reap everlasting life. And let us not grow weary while doing good, for in due season we shall reap if we do not lose heart." (See Galatians 6:8–9.)

You need to realize that when you sow the love of God, you *will* reap the love of God. You need to develop faith in this spiritual law— even though you may not harvest it from the field in which you sowed, or as quickly as you would like.

The Lord continued. "In My greatest hour of need, My closest friends deserted Me. Judas betrayed Me, Peter denied Me, and the rest fled for their lives. Only John followed from afar. I had cared for them for over three years, feeding them and teaching them. Yet as I died for the sins of the world, I forgave. I released all of them—from My friends who had deserted Me to the Roman guards who had crucified

Me. They didn't ask for forgiveness, yet I freely gave it. I had faith in the Father's love.

"I knew that because I had sown love, I would reap love from many sons and daughters of the kingdom. Because of My sacrifice of love, they would love Me.

"I said to 'love your enemies, bless those who curse you, do good to those who hate you, and pray for those who spitefully use you and persecute you, that you may be sons of your Father in heaven; for He makes His sun rise on the evil and on the good, and sends rain on the just and on the unjust.

"For if you love those who love you, what reward have you? Do not even the tax collectors do the same? And if you greet your brethren only, what do you do more than others? Do not even the tax collectors do so?'" (Matt. 5:44–47).

GREAT EXPECTATIONS

I realized that the love I was giving was being sown to the Spirit, and eventually I would reap those seeds of love. I didn't know from where, but I knew the harvest would come. No longer did I see it as a failure when love wasn't returned from the person I was giving it to. It freed me to love that person even more!

If more Christians recognized this, they wouldn't give up and become offended. Usually this is not the type of love we walk in. We walk in a selfish love that is easily disappointed when our expectations are not met.

If I have expectations about certain persons, those people can let me down. They will disappoint me to the degree that they fall short of my expectations. But if I have no expectations about someone, anything given is a blessing and not something owed. We set ourselves up for offense when we require certain behaviors from those with whom we have relationships. The more we expect, the greater the potential offense.

WALLS OF PROTECTION?

A brother offended is harder to win than a strong city, and contentions are like the bars of a castle.

—Proverbs 18:19

An offended brother or sister is harder to win than a fortified city. The strong cities had *walls* around them. These walls were the city's assurance of protection. They kept unwelcome inhabitants and invaders out. All entrants were screened. Those who owed taxes were not allowed in until they had paid. Those considered a threat to the city's health or safety were kept out.

We construct walls when we are hurt to safeguard our hearts and prevent any future wounds. We become selective, denying entry to all we fear will hurt us. We filter out anyone we think owes us something. We withhold access until these people have paid their debts in full. We open our lives only to those we believe are on our side.

Yet often these people who are "on our side" are offended as well. So, instead of helping, we stack additional stones on our existing walls. Without our knowing when it happens, these walls of protection become a prison. At that point, we are not only cautious about who comes in, but in terror we cannot venture outside our fortress.

The focus of offended Christians is inward and introspective. We guard our rights and personal relationships carefully. Our energy is consumed with making sure no future injuries will occur. If we don't risk being hurt, we cannot give unconditional love. Unconditional love gives others the *right* to hurt us.

Love does not seek its own, but hurt people become more and more self-seeking and self-contained. In this climate the love of God waxes cold. A natural example of this is the two seas in the Holy Land. The Sea of Galilee freely receives and gives out water. It has an abundance of life, nurturing many different kinds of fish and plant life. The water of the Sea of Galilee is carried by way of the Jordan River to the Dead Sea. But the Dead Sea only takes water in and does not give it out. There are no living plants or fish in it. The living waters from the Sea of Galilee become dead when mixed with the hoarded waters of the Dead Sea. Life cannot be sustained if held on to: It must be given freely.

So an offended Christian is one who takes in life but, because of fear, cannot release life. As a result, even the life that does come in becomes stagnant within the wall or prison of offense. The New Testament describes these walls as strongholds.

> For the weapons of our warfare are not carnal but mighty in God for pulling down strongholds, casting down arguments and every high thing that exalts itself against the knowledge of God, bringing every thought into captivity to the obedience of Christ.
>
> —2 Corinthians 10:4–5

These strongholds create set patterns of reasoning through which all incoming information is processed. Although they were originally erected for protection, they become a source of torment and distortion because they war against the *knowing* or knowledge of God.

When we filter everything through past hurts, rejections, and experiences, we find it impossible to believe God. We cannot believe He means what He says. We doubt His goodness and faithfulness since we judge Him by the standards set by man in our lives. *But God is not a man!* He cannot lie (Num. 23:19). His ways are not like ours, and His thoughts are not ours (Isa. 55:8–9).

Offended people will be able to find Scripture passages to back their position, but it is not the correct division of God's Word. The knowledge of God's Word without love is a destructive force because it puffs us up with pride and legalism (1 Cor. 8:1–3). This causes us to justify ourselves rather than repent of the unforgiveness.

This creates an atmosphere in which we can be deceived, because knowledge without the love of God will lead to deception.

Jesus warns of false prophets immediately after His statement of many being offended: "Then many false prophets will rise up and deceive many" (Matt. 24:11). Who are the many they will deceive? The answer: the offended whose love has grown cold (Matt. 24:12).

FALSE PROPHETS

Jesus calls false prophets "wolves in sheep's clothing" (Matt. 7:15). They are self-seeking men who give the appearance of being Christians (sheep's clothing) but have the inward nature of a wolf. Wolves like to hang around sheep. They can be found in the congregation as well as in the pulpit. They are sent by the enemy to infiltrate and deceive. They must be identified by their fruits, not by their teachings or prophecies. Often the teaching can appear sound whereas the fruit in their lives and ministries is not. A minister or a Christian is *what he lives,* not what he preaches.

Wolves always go after the wounded and young sheep, not the healthy, strong ones. These wolves will tell people what they *want* to hear, not what they *need* to hear. These people don't want sound doctrine; they want someone to tickle their ears. Let's look at what Paul says about the last days:

> But know this, that in the last days perilous times will come: For men will be... *unforgiving... having a form of godliness but denying its power.* And from such people turn away!...For the time will come when they will not endure sound doctrine, but according to their own desires, because they have itching ears, they will heap up for themselves teachers; and they will turn their ears away from the truth.
>
> —2 Timothy 3:1–5; 4:3–4, emphasis added

Notice that they will have a form of godliness or "Christianity," but they will deny its power. How will they deny its power? They deny that Christianity can change them from being unforgiving to forgiving. They will boast of being followers of Jesus and proclaim their "new birth" experience, but what they boast of has not been allowed to pierce their hearts and bring forth the character of Christ.

INFORMATION GENERATION

Paul could see prophetically that these deceived men and women would have a zeal for knowledge but remain unchanged since they never apply it. He described them as "always learning and never able to come to the knowledge of the truth" (2 Tim. 3:7).

If Paul were alive today he would grieve to see what he foretold in operation. He would see multitudes of men and women attending camp meetings, seminars, and church services amassing a knowledge of the Scriptures. He would watch them hunt for "new revelation" in order to live more selfish, successful lives. He'd see ministers taking one another to court for "righteous causes."

He would see Christian publications and radio broadcasts attacking men and women of God by name. He would see charismatics running from church to church to escape offense, all of them professing the lordship of Jesus while they cannot forgive. Paul would cry out, "Repent and be free from your deception, you self-seeking generation of hypocrites!"

It doesn't matter how up-to-date you are in new revelations from the many seminars and Bible schools you've attended or how many books you've read or even how many hours you pray and study. If you are offended and in unforgiveness and refuse to repent of this sin, you have not come to the knowledge of the truth. You are deceived, and you confuse others with your hypocritical lifestyle. No matter what the revelation, your fruit tells a different story. You'll become a spring spewing out bitter waters that will bring deception, not truth.

BETRAYAL

And then many will be *offended,* will *betray* one another, and will *hate* one another.

—MATTHEW 24:10, EMPHASIS ADDED

Let's examine this statement. If we look closely we can see a progression. An offense leads to betrayal, and betrayal leads to hatred.

As stated earlier, offended people build walls for protection. Our focus becomes self-preservation. We must be protected and safe at all costs. This makes us capable of betrayal. When we betray, we seek our own protection or benefit at the expense of someone else—usually someone with whom we are in relationship.

Thus, a betrayal in the kingdom of God comes when a believer seeks his own benefit or protection at the expense of another believer. The closer the relation, the more severe the betrayal. To betray someone is the ultimate abandonment of covenant. When betrayal occurs, the relationship cannot be restored unless genuine repentance follows.

Betrayal then leads to hatred with serious consequences. The Bible states clearly that anyone who hates his brother is a murderer and that no murderer has eternal life abiding in him (1 John 3:15).

How sad that we can find example after example of offense, betrayal, and hatred among believers today. It is so rampant in our homes and churches that it is considered normal behavior. We are too numb to grieve when we see minister taking minister to court. It no longer surprises us when Christian couples sue one another for divorce. Church splits are common and predictable. Ministry politics are played at an all-time high. It is disguised as being in the best interest of the kingdom or the church.

"Christians" are protecting their rights, making sure they are not mistreated or taken advantage of by other Christians. Have we forgotten the exhortation of the new covenant?

> Why do you not rather accept wrong? Why do you not rather let yourselves be cheated?
>
> —1 CORINTHIANS 6:7

Have we forgotten the words of Jesus?

> But I say to you, love your enemies, bless those who curse you, do good to those who hate you, and pray for those who spitefully use you and persecute you.
>
> —MATTHEW 5:44

Have we forgotten the command of God?

> Let nothing be done through selfish ambition or conceit, but in lowliness of mind let each esteem others better than himself.
>
> —PHILIPPIANS 2:3

Why don't we live by these laws of love? Why are we so quick to betray rather than lay down our lives for one another, even at the risk of being cheated? The reason: Our love is cold, which results in our still seeking to protect ourselves. We can no longer confidently commit our care to God when we are trying to care for ourselves.

When Jesus was wronged, He did not wrong in return but committed His soul to God, who would judge righteously. We are admonished to follow His steps.

> For to this you were called, because Christ also suffered for us, leaving us an example, that you should follow His steps: "Who committed no sin, nor was deceit found in His mouth"; who, when He was reviled, did not revile in return; when He suffered, He did not threaten, but committed Himself to Him who judges righteously.
>
> —1 PETER 2:21–23

THE ENABLER

We must come to the place where we trust God and not flesh. Many give lip service to God as their source, yet they live as orphans. They take their own lives in their hands while they confess with their mouths, "He is my Lord and God."

By now you see how serious the *sin* of offense is. If it is not dealt with, offense will eventually lead to death. But when you resist the temptation to be offended, God brings great victory.

IF THE DEVIL
COULD DESTROY US
WHENEVER HE WANTED TO,
HE WOULD HAVE WIPED US OUT
A LONG TIME AGO.

Before I read the book I was at a point of noncommunication with God. I was saved, but there was something between God and myself that was not quite right. I knew the loss was not on the Lord's part, but I just did not know what the problem was. I was at a friend's house one day, and she had *The Bait of Satan* by John Bevere. I brought it home and started reading it; I couldn't put the book down. It had an anointing so great my spirit was just eating it up. About halfway through the book I suddenly realized that the very thing that was standing between my relationship with the Lord was a spirit of offense.

—C. C., GEORGIA

CHAPTER 3

HOW COULD

THIS HAPPEN TO ME?

*Joseph said to them... "But as for you, you meant
evil against me; but God meant it for good."*
—GENESIS 50:19–20

IN THE FIRST CHAPTER WE GROUPED ALL OFFENDED PEOPLE INTO
two major categories: (1) those who have been genuinely mistreated
and (2) those who think they have been mistreated but actually were
not. In this chapter I want to address this first category.

Let's begin by asking a question: If you've been genuinely mistreated, do you have the right to be offended? In answer, let's look at
the life of Jacob's favorite son, Joseph. (See Genesis 37–48.)

THE DREAM BECOMES A NIGHTMARE

Joseph was Jacob's eleventh son. He was despised by his older brothers
because his father favored him and had set him apart with a coat of
many colors. God gave Joseph two dreams. In the first he saw bound
sheaves in a field. His sheaf arose and stood upright while his brothers'
sheaves bowed down to it. In the second dream he saw the sun, moon,
and eleven stars (representing his father, mother, and brothers) bowing

to him. When he told these dreams to his brothers, needless to say, they did not share in his enthusiasm. They just hated him even more.

Shortly afterward, his ten older brothers went to feed their father's flocks in the field. Jacob sent Joseph to see how they were doing. When the older brothers saw Joseph coming, they conspired against him, saying, "Here comes that dreamer. Let's kill him! Then we shall see what will become of his dreams! He says he is going to be a leader over us. Let him try to lead us when he is dead!" So they threw him in a pit to die. They took his coat away, tore it, and stained it with animal's blood to convince their father he'd been devoured by a wild beast.

After they threw him into the pit, however, they saw a company of Ishmaelites on their way to Egypt. Then Judah said, "Hey, wait a minute, guys. If we let him rot in that pit it will not profit us. Let's make some money and sell him as a slave. He will be as good as dead and will never again bother us, and we'll all share the spoils!" So they sold him for twenty shekels of silver. Joseph had offended them so they betrayed him, taking away his inheritance and family. Keep in mind these are *brothers* who did this—same father, same flesh and blood.

Now as Americans our culture is so different that it is hard for us to understand the severity of what these men did. Only killing him would have been worse. In biblical times it was very important to have sons. A man's sons carried his name and inherited all he had. Joseph's brothers kept him from ever receiving his father's name and inheritance. They blotted his name out, completely stripping him of his identity. All that was familiar to Joseph was gone.

When a person was sold as a slave to another country, he remained a slave until he died. The woman he married would be a slave, and all his children would be slaves!

It would have been hard to be born a slave, but it was indescribably worse to be born an heir of wealth with a great future only to have it stripped away. It would have been easier if Joseph never knew what could have been. It was as if he were a living dead man. I'm sure he was tempted to wish his brothers had killed him. The point is that what Joseph's brothers did was evil and cruel.

PERFECT HINDSIGHT

As you read my paraphrase of Joseph's story, you probably already knew the outcome. It is a very inspiring story when you know the ending. But that is not how Joseph experienced it. It looked as if he would never see his father or his God-given dream fulfilled. He was a slave in a foreign nation. He couldn't leave Egypt. He was the property of another man for life.

Joseph was sold to a man named Potiphar, an officer of Pharaoh and captain of the guard. He served him for about ten years. He never had word from his family, and he knew that his father believed he was dead. Their lives had gone on without him. Joseph had no hope of a father's rescue.

As time went on, Joseph found favor with his master and was treated well. Potiphar set Joseph over his household and all he had.

But at the same time that conditions were looking up for Joseph, something very wrong was brewing in the wife of his master. She had cast longing eyes on him and wanted to commit adultery with him. She tried daily to seduce him, and he refused. One day she was alone with him in the house and cornered him and insisted that he lie with her. He refused and ran out, leaving his robe in her clutched hand. When he did this she was shamed and screamed, "Rape!" Potiphar had Joseph thrown in Pharaoh's prison.

Now Pharaoh's prison was nothing like our prisons in America. I have ministered in several prisons, and as unpleasant as they are, they would be country clubs compared to this dungeon of Pharaoh. No sunlight or workout areas, just a sunken room or pit void of light and warmth. Conditions ranged from crude to dehumanizing. Prisoners were put there to rot as they survived on the bread and water "of affliction" (1 Kings 22:27). They were given just enough food to survive so they could suffer. According to Psalm 105:18, Joseph's feet were hurt with fetters, and he was laid in irons. He was put in this dungeon to die.

If he had been an Egyptian, he might have had some chance of release, but as a foreign slave, accused of rape, he had little or no hope. Things couldn't have gotten any worse. Joseph had gone as low as a person could go without being dead.

Can you hear his thoughts in the damp darkness of that dungeon? "I served my master with honesty and with integrity for over ten years. I'm more faithful than his wife. I stayed loyal to God and my master, daily fleeing sexual immorality. What is my reward? A dungeon!

"It seems that the more I try to do what is right, the worse it gets! How could God allow this? Could my brothers steal my promise from God too? Why hasn't this mighty, covenant God intervened on my behalf? Is this how a loving, faithful God cares for His servants? Why me? What have I done to deserve this? I only believed I'd heard from God."

I'm sure he wrestled with these or similar thoughts.

He had very limited freedom in his life, but he still had the right to choose his response to all that had happened to him. Would he become offended and bitter toward his brothers and eventually God? Would he give up all hope of the promise's fulfillment, robbing himself of his last incentive to live?

Is God in control?

I imagine it never crossed Joseph's mind until it was all over that this was God's process to prepare him to rule. How would he use his future authority over these brothers who betrayed him? Joseph was learning obedience by what he suffered. His brothers were skillfully wielded instruments in the hand of God. Would Joseph hold fast to the promise, seeking God for its purpose?

Perhaps when Joseph had his dreams he saw them as a confirmation of the favor on his life. He had not yet learned that authority is given to serve, not to set you apart. Often in these training periods we focus on the impossibility of our circumstances instead of the greatness of God. As a result we are discouraged and need to blame someone, so we look for the one we feel is responsible for our despair. When we face the fact that God could have prevented our whole mess—and didn't—we often blame Him.

This kept ringing through Joseph's mind: "I have lived in accordance to what I know of God. I've not transgressed His statutes or nature. I was only repeating a dream God Himself gave me. And what's the result? My brothers betray me, and I'm sold as a slave! My dad thinks I'm dead and never comes to Egypt to find me."

To him the bottom line was his brothers. They were the force that had thrown him into this dungeon. Maybe he entertained thoughts of how things would be different once he was in power, when God put him in the position of authority he had seen in the dreams. How different it all would be if his brothers had not aborted his future.

How often do we hear our brothers and sisters fall into the same trap of assigning blame? For example:

"If it weren't for my wife I would be in the ministry. She has hindered me and ruined so much of what I have dreamed."

"If it weren't for my parents I would have had a normal life. They are to blame for where I am today. How come others have normal parents and I don't? If my mom and dad didn't get divorced I would have been much better off in my own marriage."

"If it weren't for my pastor repressing this gift in me I would be free and unhindered. He has kept me from fulfilling my ministry destiny. He has turned the people in the church against me."

"If it weren't for my former husband, my kids and I wouldn't have all this financial trouble."

"If it weren't for that woman in the church I would still be in favor with the leaders. With her gossip, she has destroyed me and any hope I had of being respected."

The list is endless. It is easy to blame everyone else for the problems you have and imagine how much better off you would be if it had not been for all those around you. You know that your disappointment and hurt are their fault.

I want to emphasize the following point: *Absolutely no man, woman, child, or devil can ever get you out of the will of God! No one but God holds your destiny.* Joseph's brothers tried hard to destroy the vision God gave him. They thought they had ended it for Joseph. They said out of their own mouths, "Come, therefore, let us now kill him and cast him into some pit.... *We shall see what will become of his dreams!*" (Gen. 37:20, emphasis added). They were out to destroy him. It wasn't an accident. It was deliberate! They wanted no chance of his ever succeeding.

Now do you think that when they sold him as a slave, God in heaven looked at the Son and the Holy Spirit and said, "What are We going to do now? Look at what his brothers have done. They have ruined Our plan for Joseph. We had better think of something quick! Do We have an alternate plan?"

Many Christians respond to crisis situations as if this is exactly what transpires in heaven. Can you just see the Father saying to Jesus, "Jesus, Jim just got fired because a fellow believer lied about him. What are We going to do? Do You have any positions open down there?" Or, "Jesus, Sally is thirty-four and not married yet. Do You have any available guys down there for her? The man I wanted her to marry got married to her best friend, who gossiped about her and turned his heart away." It sounds absurd, yet the way we react insinuates that this is the way we view God.

Let's see how Joseph would fare in our churches today. If he were like most of us, do you know what he would be doing? Plotting revenge. He would comfort himself with such thoughts as, "When I get my hands on them, I'll kill them! I will kill them for what they have done to me. They are going to pay for this."

But if Joseph had actually had this attitude, God would have left him in that dungeon to rot! That's because if he had gotten out of prison with this motive, he would have killed the heads of ten of the twelve tribes of Israel. This would include Judah, from whose lineage Christ would descend.

Yes, the ones who treated Joseph so wickedly were the patriarchs of Israel! And God had promised Abraham that they would bring forth a nation. Through them the Lord Jesus would eventually come! Joseph stayed free from offense, and the plan of God was established in his life and in the lives of his brothers.

COULD IT GET ANY WORSE?

Prison was a time of sifting for Joseph, but it was also a time of opportunity. There were two prisoners with Joseph, and both had vivid and disturbing dreams. Joseph interpreted both of their dreams with amazing accuracy. One man was to be restored while the other would be executed. Joseph asked the one about to be restored to remember him when he regained Pharaoh's favor. The man returned to Pharaoh's service, but two years passed with no word from him. It was yet another letdown for Joseph, another opportunity to become offended.

God always has a plan.

The time came when Pharaoh had a very alarming dream. None of his magicians or wise men could give him the explanation. It was then that the restored servant remembered Joseph. He shared how Joseph had interpreted his and his companion's dreams in prison. Joseph was brought before Pharaoh, and he told him what the dream meant—a famine was coming—and wisely instructed him on how to prepare for the crisis. Pharaoh immediately promoted Joseph to second in command over all of Egypt. Joseph, through the wisdom God had given him, prepared for the severe famine that was coming.

Later when this famine came to all the known nations, Joseph's brothers had to come to Egypt for aid. If Joseph had held anything in his heart against his brothers, that would have been the time to carry it out. He could have thrown them in prison for life or tortured them and even killed them and not be blamed because he was second in command in Egypt. His brothers were of no concern to Pharaoh.

But Joseph ended up giving them grain for no charge. Then they were given the best land of Egypt for their families, and they ate the fat of the land. To sum it up, the best of all the land of Egypt was given to them. Joseph ended up blessing those who had cursed him and doing good to those who hated him. (See Matthew 5:44.)

God knew what Joseph's brothers would do before they did it. As a matter of fact, the Lord knew they would do it before He gave Joseph the dream or before any of those boys was born.

To go one step further, look at what Joseph said to his brothers when they were reunited. "But now, do not therefore be grieved or angry with yourselves because you sold me here; *for God sent me* before you to preserve life. For these two years the famine has been in the land, and there are still five years in which there will be neither plowing nor harvesting. And *God sent me* before you to preserve a posterity for you in the earth, and to save your lives by a great deliverance. *So now it was not you who sent me here, but God*" (Gen. 45:5–8, emphasis added).

Look at what the psalmist said: "Moreover He [God] called for a famine in the land; He destroyed all the provision of bread. *He sent a man before them—Joseph—who was sold as a slave*" (Ps. 105:16–17, emphasis added).

Who sent Joseph? His brothers or God? Out of the mouth of two witnesses we see that it was God who sent him. Joseph said plainly to his brothers, "It was not you who sent me." Hear what the Spirit is saying!

As already stated, no mortal man or devil can supersede the plan of God for your life. If you lay hold of this truth, it will set you free. But there is only one person who can get you out of the will of God, and that is you!

Consider the children of Israel. God had sent a deliverer, Moses, to lead them out of Egyptian bondage into the Promised Land. After a year in the desert, leaders were sent to spy it out. They returned complaining. They were afraid of the nations in the land who were larger and stronger militarily.

All the people, with the exception of Joshua and Caleb, agreed with these leaders. The people felt as if God had brought them out to die. They were offended with Moses and God. This pattern had been going on for over a year. Their offense resulted in that generation's never seeing the land God promised they would possess.

Many people have been serving the Lord fervently and have come into difficult life situations because of being mistreated by either wicked men or carnal Christians. The truth is that they *have* been treated unjustly. But to become offended would only fulfill the enemy's purpose of getting them out of the will of God.

If you stay free from offense you will stay in God's will. If you become offended you will be taken captive by the enemy to fulfill his own purpose and will. Take your pick. It is much more beneficial to stay free from offense.

We must remember that nothing can come against us without the Lord's knowledge of it before it ever happens. If the devil could destroy us at will, he would have wiped us out a long time ago because he hates man with a passion. Always keep this exhortation before you:

No temptation has overtaken you except such as is common to man; but God is faithful, who will not allow you to be tempted beyond what you are able, but with the temptation will also make *the way of escape,* that you may be able to bear it.

—1 Corinthians 10:13, emphasis added

Notice it says "*the* way of escape," not "a way of escape." God has already seen every adverse circumstance we will encounter—no matter how great or small—and He has *the* way planned for escaping it. And, even more thrilling, often the thing that looks like an abortion of God's plan actually ends up being the road to its fulfillment if we stay in obedience and free from offense.

So remember: Stay submitted to God by not becoming offended; resist the devil, and he will flee from you (James 4:7). We resist the devil by not becoming offended. The dream or vision will probably happen differently than how you think it will, but His Word and His promises will not fail. We only risk aborting them by our disobedience.

ANOTHER KIND OF BETRAYAL

Not many have suffered the treatment Joseph received from his brothers. It would not have been as painful if his *enemies* did this. But these were his *brothers*, his flesh and blood. They were the ones who were supposed to encourage, support, defend, and care for him. Could there be a worse scenario of mistreatment than that which Joseph endured?

IT IS ONE THING TO
EXPERIENCE REJECTION AND
MALICE FROM A BROTHER OR SISTER,
BUT IT IS ENTIRELY DIFFERENT TO
EXPERIENCE REJECTION AND
MALICE FROM A FATHER.

I am a multigrade junior high and high school teacher. I recently read *The Bait of Satan,* which brought several revelations to my life. I shared the video with my students, and the Holy Ghost was so strong in our classroom that everyone began to confess offenses and ask for forgiveness. Several students said that was the best day they had all year. One student reconciled with her father after a huge falling out; another started the healing process from deep wounds with her grandmother. The Lord really ministered to these students in a mighty way. Thank you for this message.

—R. F., INDIANA

Chapter 4

MY FATHER, MY FATHER!

My father...know and see that there is neither evil
nor rebellion in my hand, and I have not sinned
against you. Yet you hunt my life to take it.
—1 Samuel 24:11

In the last chapter we saw how Joseph's brothers sought to destroy him. We saw the pain he experienced from this betrayal. Perhaps you're in a similar situation. You've been betrayed by those closest to you, people from whom you wanted love and encouragement.

In this chapter I want to deal with a situation more painful than a betrayal by a brother. It is one thing to experience rejection and malice from a brother, but it is entirely different to experience rejection and malice from a father. When I speak of fathers, I am not just referring to a biological father but to any leader God puts over us. These are the people we thought would love, train, nurture, and care for us.

A LOVE-HATE RELATIONSHIP

To examine an example of a father who betrayed, let's look at the relationship between King Saul and David. (See 1 Samuel 16–31.) Their lives touched even before they met, as Samuel, the prophet of God, anointed David to be the next king of Israel. David must have been overwhelmed with excitement, thinking, "This is the same man who anointed Saul. I am really going to be king!"

Back at the palace, Saul was being tormented by an evil spirit because he had disobeyed God. His only relief came as someone played the harp. Saul's servants began to look for a young man who could sit in his presence and minister to him. One of the king's servants suggested David, the son of Jesse. King Saul sent for David and asked him to come to the palace and minister to him.

David must have thought, "God is already bringing to pass His promise through the prophet. Surely I'll win the favor of the king. This must be my entry-level position."

Time passed, and David's father asked him to bring refreshments to his older brothers, who were at war with the Philistines. Upon arriving at the battle lines, David saw the Philistine champion, Goliath, mocking the army of God and learned that this had gone on for forty days. He found out that the king had offered his daughter's hand in marriage to the man who defeated this giant.

David went before the king and requested permission to fight. He killed Goliath and won Saul's daughter. By then he had won Saul's favor and was brought into the palace to live with the king. Jonathan, Saul's oldest son, made a covenant of everlasting friendship with David. In everything Saul gave David to do, the hand of God was on him, and it prospered. The king requested that he eat at the table with his own sons.

David was thrilled. He was living in the palace, eating at the king's table, married to the king's daughter, friends with Jonathan, and successful in all his campaigns. He was even winning the favor of the people. He could see the prophecy unfolding before his very eyes.

Saul favored David over all his other servants. He had become a father to him. David was sure Saul would mentor and train him and one day, with great honor, put him on the throne. David was rejoicing in God's faithfulness and goodness.

But in one day everything changed.

As Saul and David returned from battle, side by side, the women from all the cities of Israel came out dancing and singing: "Saul has slain his thousands, and David his ten thousands." This infuriated Saul, and from that day forward he despised David. Twice, as David played his harp for him, Saul tried to kill him.

The Bible says that Saul hated David because he knew God was with David but not with him. David was forced to run for his life. With nowhere else to go, he ran to the wilderness.

"What is happening?" David wondered. "The promise was unfolding, and now it is shattered. The man who is my mentor is trying to kill me. What can I do? Saul is God's anointed servant. With him against me, what chance do I have? He's the king, God's man, over God's nation. Why is God allowing this?"

Saul chased David from wilderness to wilderness and cave to cave, accompanied by three thousand of Israel's finest warriors. They had one purpose: to destroy David.

At this point the promise was just a shadow. David no longer lived at the palace nor ate at the king's table. He inhabited damp caves and ate the scraps of wilderness beasts. He no longer rode at the king's side but was hunted by the men who once fought by his side. There was no warm bed or servants to attend him, no compliments in the royal court. His bride was given to another. He knew the loneliness of a man without a country.

Notice that God, not the devil, placed David under the care of Saul. Why would God not only allow this but also plan it? Why was favor dangled before David's eyes only to have it abruptly taken away? This was a prime opportunity for David to be offended—not only with Saul but also with God. All the unanswered questions increased the temptation to question God's wisdom and plan.

Saul was so determined to kill this young man, at any cost, that his madness increased. He became a desperate man. Priests in the city of Nob provided David with shelter, food, and Goliath's sword. They knew nothing about David's running from Saul and thought he was on a mission for the king. They inquired of the Lord on David's behalf and sent him on his way.

When Saul found out, he was furious. He killed eighty-five innocent priests of the Lord and put the entire city of Nob to the sword—every man, woman, child, nursing infant, cow, donkey, and sheep. He carried the judgment against them—the innocent—that he was supposed to carry against the Amalekites. He was a murderer. How could God have ever put His Spirit on such a man?

At one point Saul learned David was in the wilderness of En Gedi and set out after him with three thousand warriors. During their journey they stopped to rest at the entrance of a cave, not knowing that David was hiding in the back. Saul removed his outer robe and laid it aside. David quietly slipped out of his hiding place, cut off a piece of the discarded robe, and crept away without being noticed.

After Saul left the cave, David bowed down to the ground and cried out after him: "My father, see! Yes, see the corner of your robe in my hand!…know and see that there is *neither evil nor rebellion* in my hand, and I have not sinned against you. Yet you hunt my life to take it" (1 Sam. 24:11, emphasis added).

David's cry to Saul was, "My father, my father!" To put it plainly, he was crying, "See my heart! Be a father to me. I need a leader to train me, not to destroy me!" Even while Saul was trying to kill him, David's heart still burned with hope.

WHERE ARE THE FATHERS?

I have seen this cry in countless men and women in the body of Christ. Most of them are young and with a strong call of God on their lives. They cry out for a father, a man to disciple, love, support, and encourage them. This is why God said He would "turn the hearts of the fathers [leaders] to the children [people], and the hearts of the children to their fathers, lest I come and strike the earth with a curse" (Mal. 4:6).

Our nation lost its fathers (dads, leaders, or ministers) in the 1940s and 1950s, and today our condition is getting worse. Not unlike Saul, many leaders in our homes, corporations, and churches are more concerned with their goals than with their offspring.

Because of this attitude, these leaders view God's people as resources to serve their vision instead of seeing the vision as the vehicle to serve the people. The success of the vision justifies the cost of wounded lives and shattered people. Justice, mercy, integrity, and love are compromised for success. Decisions are based on money, numbers, and results.

This opens the door to treatment such as David received—after all, Saul had a kingdom to protect. This type of treatment is acceptable in the leaders' minds because they are pursuing the furtherance of the gospel.

How many leaders have cut off men under them because of suspicion? Why are those leaders suspicious? Because they are not serving God. They are serving a vision. Like Saul, they are insecure in their calling, and that breeds jealousy and pride. They recognize qualities in people that they know are godly, and they are willing to use those people as long as it benefits them. Saul enjoyed the success of David until he saw it as a threat to him. He then demoted David and watched for a reason to destroy him.

I have talked with countless young men and women who cried out for accountability. They wanted to be submitted to a leader who would disciple them. They felt isolated and alone. They were seeking someone to father them. But God allowed them to go through rejection because God wanted to do in them what He had done in David. Listen carefully to what the Spirit is saying.

David was concerned that Saul believed he was rebellious and evil. David must have searched his heart, saying, "Where have I gone wrong? How was Saul's heart turned against me so quickly?" That is why he cried out, "Someone urged me to kill you, but I said no. I only cut off the corner of your robe so that you could *know and see that there is neither evil nor rebellion in my hand.*" (See 1 Samuel 24:11.) David thought if he could prove his love for Saul, Saul would restore him to favor, and the prophecy would be fulfilled.

People who have been rejected by a father or leader tend to take all the blame on themselves. They are imprisoned by tormenting thoughts of "What did I do?" and "Was my heart impure?" They sometimes wonder, "Who turned the heart of my leader against me?" Then they constantly try to prove their innocence to their leaders. They think that if they can only show their loyalty and value they will be accepted. Sadly, the more they try, the more rejected they feel.

WHO WILL AVENGE ME?

Saul acknowledged David's goodness when he saw David could have killed him and did not. So he and his men left. David must have thought, "Now the king will restore me. Now the prophecy will come to pass. Surely he sees my heart and will treat me better now."

Not so fast, David. Only a short time later, men reported to Saul that David was in the hills of Hachilah. Saul went after him again with the same three thousand soldiers. I'm sure this devastated David. He realized it wasn't a misunderstanding but that Saul was intentionally, without provocation, seeking his life. How rejected he must have felt. Saul knew his heart and still marched against him.

David, along with Abishai, slipped into Saul's camp. Not one guard saw them because God had put them all in a deep sleep. These two men sneaked through the entire army to where Saul was sleeping.

Abishai pleaded with David. "God has delivered your enemy into your hand this day. Now therefore, please, let me strike him at once with the spear, right to the earth; and I will not have to strike him a second time!" (1 Sam. 26:8).

Abishai had very good reasons why he thought David should allow him to kill Saul. First, Saul had murdered eighty-five innocent priests and their families—in cold blood!

Second, he was out with an army of three thousand to kill David and his followers. If you don't kill the enemy first, Abishai reasoned, he will surely kill you. It is self-defense. Every court of law allows for that!

Third, God through Samuel had anointed David as the next king of Israel. David should claim his inheritance if he didn't want to end up a dead man without the prophecy ever being fulfilled.

Fourth, God put this entire army into a deep sleep so that David and Abishai could walk right up to Saul. Why else would God do this? To Abishai it seemed David would never get a chance like this again.

All these reasons sounded good. They made sense, and David was receiving the encouragement from another brother. So if David was the least bit offended, he would have felt totally justified and would have allowed Abishai to put a spear through Saul.

Listen to David's response: "Do not destroy him; for who can stretch out his hand against the LORD's anointed, and be guiltless?...as the LORD lives, the LORD shall strike him, or his day shall come to die, or he shall go out to battle and perish. The LORD forbid that I should stretch out my hand against the LORD's anointed" (1 Sam. 26:9–11, emphasis added).

David would not kill Saul even though Saul had murdered innocent people and wanted to murder David as well. David would not avenge himself, but he left it in the hands of God.

Of course, it would have been easier to put an end to it right there—easy for David *and* for the people of Israel. He knew the nation was like a flock of sheep without a shepherd. He knew a wolf was robbing them for his own selfish desires. It was hard for him not to defend himself, but it was possibly harder not to deliver the people he loved from a mad king. David made this decision even though he knew Saul's only comfort was the thought of his destruction.

David had proved his purity of heart when he spared Saul the first time. Yet even when David had a second chance to kill Saul, he would not touch him. Saul was anointed of the Lord, and David left him in God's hand to judge.

How many people today have a heart like David's? We no longer kill with physical swords but ravage each other with a sword of another kind—the tongue. "Death and life are in the power of the tongue" (Prov. 18:21).

Churches split, families divide, marriages shatter, and love dies, crushed by an onslaught of words launched in hurt and frustration. Offended by friends, family, and leaders, we take aim with words sharpened by bitterness and anger. Even though information may be factual and accurate, motives are impure.

Proverbs 6:16–19 says that sowing discord or separation among brethren is an abomination to the Lord. When we repeat something with the intention of separating or damaging relationships or reputations—even though it is true—it is still an affront to God.

IS GOD USING ME TO EXPOSE MY LEADER'S SINS?

For seven years I served full-time in the ministry of helps and pastored youth before God released my wife and me to our present ministry. While I was a youth pastor, there was a man who did not like me or the message I preached. Normally that would not bother me, but this man had a position of authority over me.

I believed God had told me to bring a strong word of purity and boldness to the young people, and his son was in my group.

Conviction was stirring in this young man's heart. One day he came to us crying. He was upset because he felt the lifestyle he saw at home fell short of what I was challenging him and the other young people to follow.

This incident and other personality conflicts seemed to make his father determined to get rid of me. He would go to the head pastor to stir his anger against me with false accusations. Then he would turn around and tell me how the senior pastor was against me but that he was standing up for me. There were assorted critical staff memos, none that bore my name, but they identified me in other ways. He would smile to my face, but his intention was to destroy me.

Several members of the youth group said they had heard I was to be fired. It was this man's son spreading the news, not in a malicious way, but just because he was repeating what he'd heard at home. I was angry and confused. I went to this man, and he admitted saying this, but he said he was just repeating the senior pastor's thoughts.

Months went by, and there seemed to be no way to alleviate the situation. He had even severed all contact between my senior pastor and me. This was not only the case for me but for all the pastors that were not in his favor.

My family was under constant pressure, never knowing whether we would remain at the church or be put out. We had bought a house, my wife was pregnant, and we had nowhere to go. I did not want to send out résumés. I believed God had brought me to that church, and I was staying with no plan B.

My wife was a nervous wreck. "Honey, I know they are going to fire you. Everyone is telling me they are."

"They didn't hire me, and they can't fire me without God's approval," I told her. She thought I was denying the circumstances and begged me to quit.

Finally the news came that the decision to fire me had been made. The senior pastor announced to the church that changes were coming to the youth group. I still had not spoken with him about the conflict with the leader he had put over me. I was scheduled to meet with him and that man the next day. God very specifically impressed upon me not to defend myself.

When I met with my pastor the next day, I was surprised to find the pastor sitting alone in his office. He looked at me and said, "John, God sent you to this church. I am not letting you go."

I was relieved. God had protected me at the last moment.

"Why is this man after you?" he asked me. "Please go to him and make it right between you and him."

Shortly after that meeting I received written evidence of a decision the leader had made regarding my area of responsibility. It exposed his true motives. I was ready to take it to the senior pastor.

That day I paced the floor and prayed for forty-five minutes, trying to overcome the uncomfortable feeling I had. I kept saying, "God, this man has been dishonest and wicked. He must be exposed. He is a destructive force in this ministry. I must tell the pastor the way he really is!"

I further justified my intentions to expose him. "Everything I am reporting is fact and documented, not emotional. If he is not stopped, his wickedness will infiltrate this entire church."

Finally, in frustration, I blurted out, "God, You don't want me to expose him, do You?"

When I spoke those words, the peace of God flooded my heart. I shook my head in amazement. I knew God did not want me to do anything, so I threw away the evidence. Later, when I could look at the scene more objectively, I realized I had wanted to avenge myself more than protect anyone in the ministry. I had reasoned myself into believing my motives were unselfish. My information was accurate, but my motives were impure.

Time passed, and one day as I was praying outside the church before office hours, the man drove up to the church. God impressed upon me to go to him and humble myself. Immediately I was defensive. "No, Lord, he needs to come to me. He is the one causing all the problems."

I continued to pray, but again the Lord insisted that I go to him immediately and humble myself. I knew it was God. I phoned him from my office and went to his. But what I said and how I said it was much different from how it would have been if God hadn't dealt with me.

With all sincerity I asked his forgiveness. "I have been critical and judgmental of you," I confessed.

He immediately softened, and we talked for an hour. From that day forward his attacks against me stopped, even though a problem continued between him and some of the other pastors.

41

Six months later, while I was ministering out of the country, all the wrong this man had done was exposed to the senior pastor. It had nothing to do with me but with other areas of the ministry. What he was doing was much worse than what I knew. He was fired immediately.

Judgment had come, but not by my hand. The very thing he tried to do to me happened to him. However, when it happened to him, I was not happy. I grieved for him and his family. I understood his pain—I had gone through it myself at his hands.

Because I had forgiven him six months previously, I now loved him and did not wish this for him. If he had been fired when I was angry with him a year earlier, I would have rejoiced. I knew then I was truly free from the offense I'd harbored. Humility and refusing to avenge myself were the keys that freed me from my prison of offense.

A year later I saw him in an airport. I was overwhelmed with the love of God. I ran over to where he was standing and hugged him. I was genuinely happy when he told me things were well with him. If I had never gone to him and humbled myself months earlier in his office, I wouldn't have been able to look him in the eye that day at the airport. Several years have passed since I've seen him, but I feel only love and a sincere desire to see him in God's will.

David was wise when he chose to let God be Saul's judge. You ask, "Whom did God use to judge Saul, His servant?" The Philistines. Saul, along with his sons, died battling them. When the news reached David, he did not celebrate. He mourned.

One man boasted to David that he had killed Saul. He had hoped this news would win his favor, but it had an opposite effect. "How was it you were not afraid to put forth your hand to destroy the Lord's anointed?" David asked. He ordered that the man be executed. (See 2 Samuel 1:14–15.)

David then composed a song for the people of Judah to sing in honor of Saul and his sons. He charged the people not to proclaim it in the streets of the Philistine cities lest the enemy rejoice. He proclaimed no rain or crops in the place where Saul was slain. He called for all of Israel to weep over Saul. This is not the heart of an offended man. An offended man would have said, "He got what he deserved!"

David went even further. He did not kill the remaining seed of the house of Saul. Instead he showed kindness to them. He gave land

and food to them and granted a descendant a seat at the king's table. Does this sound like an offended man?

Even though David was rejected by the one who should have fathered him, he remained loyal even after Saul's death. It is easy to be loyal to a leader or father who loves you, but what about one who is out to destroy you? Will you be a man or woman after the heart of God, or will you seek to avenge yourself?

IT IS RIGHTEOUS FOR
GOD TO AVENGE HIS SERVANTS.
IT IS UNRIGHTEOUS FOR GOD'S
SERVANTS TO AVENGE
THEMSELVES.

Mr. Bevere, I just read your book *The Bait of Satan* today—I could not put it down! This is certainly one of the best books I have ever read.

—P. A., MISSOURI

CHAPTER 5

HOW SPIRITUAL
VAGABONDS ARE BORN

"The LORD forbid that I should do this thing to my
master, the LORD's anointed, to stretch out my hand
against him, seeing he is the anointed of the LORD."
So David restrained his servants with these words,
and did not allow them to rise against Saul.
—1 SAMUEL 24:6–7

IN THE LAST CHAPTER WE SAW HOW DAVID WAS MISTREATED BY the man he had hoped would be his father. David kept trying to understand where he had gone wrong. What had he done to turn Saul's heart against him, and how could he win it back? He proved his loyalty by sparing Saul's life even though Saul aggressively pursued his.

He cried out to Saul with his head bowed to the ground, saying, "See that there is neither evil nor rebellion in my hand, and I have not sinned against you."

Once David knew he had shown his loyalty to his leader, his mind was eased. Later he learned more devastating news: Saul still desired to destroy him. But David refused to raise a hand against the one who sought to take his life, though God had put the army to sleep and had given him a companion who pleaded for permission to kill

Saul. David somehow sensed that this sleeping army served another purpose—the testing of his very heart.

God wanted to see whether David would kill to establish his kingdom, after the order of Saul, or allow God to establish his throne in righteousness forever.

> Beloved, do not avenge yourselves, but rather give place to wrath; for it is written, "Vengeance is Mine, I will repay," says the Lord.
> —ROMANS 12:19

It is righteous for God to avenge His servants. It is unrighteous for God's servants to avenge themselves. Saul was a man who avenged himself. He chased David, a man of honor, for fourteen years and murdered the priests and their families.

As David stood over the sleeping Saul, he faced an important test. It would reveal whether David still had the noble heart of a shepherd or the insecurity of another Saul. Would he remain a man after God's heart? Initially it is so much easier when we take matters into our own hands, rather than waiting on a righteous God.

God tests His servants with obedience. He deliberately places us in situations where the standards of religion and society would appear to justify our actions. He allows others, especially those close to us, to encourage us to protect ourselves. We may even think we would be noble and protect others by avenging ourselves. But this is not God's way. It is the way of the world's wisdom. It is earthly and fleshly.

When I consider the opportunity I had for exposing the leader over me, I remember wrestling with the thought that he might hurt others if he was not exposed. I kept thinking, "I'm only reporting truth. If I don't, how will this ever end?" I was encouraged by others to expose him.

Today, however, I know that God gave me that information for one reason—to test me. Was I going to become like the man who sought to destroy me? Or would I allow for God's judgment or mercy if the man repented?

HOW CAN GOD USE CORRUPT LEADERS?

Many people ask, "Why does God put people under leaders who make serious mistakes and even some who are wicked?"

Look at the childhood of Samuel. (See 1 Samuel 2–5.) God, not the devil, was the One who put this young man under the authority of a corrupt priest named Eli and his two wicked sons, Hophni and Phinehas, who were priests as well. These men were very wicked. They took offerings by manipulation and force, and they committed fornication with the women who assembled at the door of the tabernacle.

Can you imagine if you were serving a minister who lived this kind of life? A minister who was so insensitive to the things of the Spirit that he couldn't recognize a woman in prayer and accused her of being drunk! So fleshly that he was grossly overweight. So compromising that he did nothing about his sons, whom he had appointed as leaders, who were committing fornication right in the church.

Most Christians today would be offended and search for another church, telling others as they went of the wicked lifestyle of their former pastor and his leaders. In the midst of such corruption, I love the report of what young Samuel did: "Now the boy Samuel ministered to the LORD before Eli" (1 Sam. 3:1).

But corruption took its toll: "And the word of the Lord was rare in those days; there was no widespread revelation" (1 Sam. 3:1). God seemed distant to the entire Hebrew community. The lamp of God was about to go out in the temple of the Lord. Yet did Samuel go look for another place to worship? Did he go to the elders to expose the wickedness of Eli and his sons? Did he form a committee to put Eli and his sons out of the pastorate? No, he ministered to the Lord!

God had placed Samuel there, and he was not responsible for the behavior of Eli or his sons. He was put under them not to judge them but to serve them. He knew Eli was God's servant, not his. He knew that God was quite capable of dealing with His own.

Children do not correct fathers. But it is the duty of fathers to train and correct the children. We are to deal with and confront those whom God has given us to train. This is our responsibility. Those on our own level we are to encourage and exhort as brothers and sisters. But in this chapter, as with the last, I am dealing with our response to those in authority over us.

Samuel served God's appointed minister the best he could, without the pressure to judge him or correct him. The only time Samuel spoke a word of correction was when Eli came to Samuel and asked him what prophecy God had given him the night before. But even then it was not a word of correction from Samuel, but from God. If more people would get hold of this truth, our churches would be different.

CHURCHES AREN'T CAFETERIAS

Today men and women leave churches so readily if they see something wrong in the leadership. Perhaps it is the way the pastor takes offerings. Maybe it is the way the money is spent. If they don't like what the pastor preaches, they leave. He is either not approachable, or he is too familiar. This list doesn't end. Rather than face the difficulties and maintain hope, they run to where there appears to be no conflict.

Let's face it: Jesus is the only perfect pastor. So why do we run from difficulties in America instead of facing them and working through them? When we don't hit these conflicts head-on, we usually leave offended. Sometimes we say our prophetic ministry just was not received. We then go from church to church looking for a place with flawless leadership.

At the initial writing of this book, I had been a member of only two churches in two different states in the past fourteen years. I have had more than two—in fact, numerous—opportunities to become offended with the leadership over me (most of which, I might add, stemmed from my own fault or immaturity). I had the chance to become critical and judgmental with leadership, but leaving was not the answer. In the midst of a very trying circumstance, one day the Lord spoke to me through a Scripture verse and said, "This is the way I want you to leave a church":

> For you shall go out with joy, and be *led out with peace.*
> —ISAIAH 55:12, EMPHASIS ADDED

Most do not leave this way. They think churches are like cafeterias; they can pick and choose what they like! They feel the freedom to stay as long as there are no problems. But this does not agree at all with what the Bible teaches. You are not the one who chooses where you go to church. God does! The Bible does not say, "God has set the members, each one of them, in the body *just as they please.*" Rather it says, "But now God has set the members, each one of them, in the body *just as He pleased*" (1 Cor. 12:18, emphasis added).

Remember that, if you're in the place where God wants you, the devil will try to offend you to get you out. He wants to uproot men and women from the place where God plants them. If he can get you out, he has been successful. If you will not budge, even in the midst of great conflict, you will spoil his plans.

THE CRITICAL DECEPTION

I was in a church for several years. The pastor was one of the best preachers in America. When I first attended that church, I would sit with my mouth open in awe of the biblical teaching that came from his mouth.

As time passed, because of my position of serving the pastor, I was close enough to see his flaws. I questioned some of his ministry decisions. I became critical and judgmental, and offense set in. He preached, and I sensed no inspiration or anointing. His preaching no longer ministered to me.

Another couple who were our friends and also on staff seemed to be discerning the same thing. God sent them out from the church, and they started their own ministry. They asked us to go with them. They knew how we were struggling. They encouraged us to get on with the call on our lives. They would tell us all the things this pastor, his wife, and the leadership were doing wrong. We would commiserate together, feeling hopeless and trapped.

They seemed sincerely concerned for our welfare. But our discussion only fueled our fire of discontent and offense. As Proverbs 26:20 illustrates, "where there is no wood, the fire goes out; and where there is no talebearer, strife ceases." What they were saying to us may have been correct information, but it was wrong in the eyes of God because it was adding wood to the fire of offense in them as well as in us.

"We know you are a man of God," they said to me. "That's why you are having the problems you are having in this place." It sounded good.

My wife and I said to each other, "That is it. We are in a bad situation. We need to get out. This pastor and his wife love us. They will pastor us. The people in their church will receive us and the ministry God has given us."

We left our home church and began attending this couple's church, but only for a few short months. Even though we thought we had run from our problem, we noticed there was still a struggle for us. Our spirits had no joy. We were bound to a fear of becoming what we had just left. It seemed everything we did was forced and unnatural. We couldn't fit into the flow of the Spirit. Now even our relationship with the new pastor and his wife was strained.

Finally I knew we should return to our home church. When we did, we knew at once that we were back in the will of God, even though it had appeared that we would be more accepted and loved elsewhere.

Then God shocked me. "John, I never told you to leave this church. You left out of offense!"

This was not the fault of the other pastor and his wife, but ours. They understood our frustration and were trying to resolve the same issues in their own hearts. When you're out of the will of God, you will not be a blessing or help to any church. When you're out of the will of God, even the good relationships will be strained. We had been out of God's will.

Offended people react to the situation and do things that appear right even though they are not inspired by God. We are not called to react but to act.

If we are obedient to God and have sought Him, and He is not speaking, then do you know what the answer is? He is probably saying, "Stay right where you are. Don't change a thing."

Often, when we feel pressure, we look for a word from God to bring us relief. But God puts us in these very uncomfortable crucibles to mature, refine, and strengthen us, not to destroy us!

Within one month I had an opportunity to meet with the pastor of my original church. I repented of being critical and rebellious. He graciously forgave me. Our relationship was strengthened, and joy returned to my heart. I immediately started to receive the pastor's ministry from the pulpit again, and I remained in that church for years.

THE PLANTED FLOURISH

The Bible says in Psalm 92:13, "Those who are *planted* in the house of the LORD *shall flourish* in the courts of our God" (emphasis added).

Notice that those who flourish are "planted" in the house of the Lord. What happens to a plant if you transplant it every three weeks? Most of you know that its root system will diminish, and it will not blossom or prosper. If you keep transplanting it, the plant will die of shock!

Many people go from church to church, ministry team to ministry team, trying to develop their ministry. If God puts them in a place where they are not recognized and encouraged, they are easily offended. If they don't agree with the way something is done, they are offended and go. They then leave, blaming the leadership. They are blind to any of their own character flaws and do not realize God wanted to refine and mature them through the pressure they were under.

Let's learn from the examples God gives with plants and trees. When a fruit tree is put in the ground it has to face rainstorms, hot sun, and wind. If a young tree could talk, it might say, "Please get me out of here! Put me in a place where there is no sweltering heat or windy storms!"

If the gardener listened to the tree, he would actually harm it. Trees endure the hot sun and rainstorms by sending their roots down deeper. The adversity they face is eventually the source of great stability. The harshness of the elements surrounding them causes them to seek another source of life. They will one day come to the place that even the greatest of windstorms cannot affect their ability to produce fruit.

Several years ago I lived in Florida, a citrus capital. Most Floridians know that the colder the winter is for the trees, the sweeter the oranges. If we did not run so fast from spiritual resistance, our root systems would have a chance to become stronger and deeper, and our fruit would be plentiful and sweeter in the eyes of God and more palatable to His people! We would be mature trees that the Lord delights in, rather than ones uprooted for their lack of fruit (Luke 13:6–9). We should not resist the very thing God sends to mature us.

The psalmist David, inspired by the Holy Ghost, made a powerful connection between offense, the law of God, and our spiritual growth. He wrote in Psalm 1:

> Blessed is the man…[whose] delight is in the law of the Lord; and
> in His law he meditates day and night.
>
> —PSALM 1:1–2

Then in Psalm 119:165 he gave us more insight into people who love God's laws.

> Great peace have they which love [or delight in] thy law: and
> nothing shall *offend* them.
>
> —KJV, EMPHASIS ADDED

Verse 3 of Psalm 1 finally describes the destiny of such a person.

> He shall be like a *tree* planted by the rivers of water, that brings
> forth its fruit in its season, whose leaf also shall not wither; and
> whatever he does shall prosper.
>
> —EMPHASIS ADDED

In other words, a believer who chooses to delight in the Word of God in the midst of adversity will avoid being offended. That person will be like a tree whose roots search deep to where the Spirit provides strength and nourishment. He will draw from the well of God deep within his spirit. This will mature him to the point where adversity will now be the catalyst for fruit. Hallelujah!

Now we gain insight into Jesus's interpretation of the parable of the sower.

> And these are they likewise which are sown on stony ground; who,
> when they have heard the word, immediately receive it with glad-
> ness; and have no root in themselves, and so *endure* but for a time:
> afterward, when affliction or persecution ariseth for the word's sake,
> *immediately they are offended.*
>
> —MARK 4:16–17, KJV, EMPHASIS ADDED

Once you leave the place God has chosen for you, your root system begins to dwarf. The next time it will be easier for you to flee from adversity because you have been careful not to root yourself deeply. You end up coming to the place where you have little or no strength to endure hardship or persecution.

You then become a spiritual vagabond, wandering from place to place, suspicious and afraid that others will mistreat you. Crippled and hindered in your ability to produce true spiritual fruit, you struggle in a self-centered life, eating the remains of the fruit of others.

Look at Cain and Abel, the first sons of Adam. Cain brought an offering to the Lord from the works of his own hands, the fruit of his vineyard. It was brought forth with much toil. He had to clear the ground of rocks, stumps, and other debris. He had to plow and cultivate the soil. He had to plant, water, fertilize, and protect his crops. He put much effort in his service toward God. But it was his own sacrifice rather than obedience toward God's way. It symbolized the worship of God by one's own strength and ability rather than by God's grace.

Abel, on the other hand, brought an offering of obedience, the choice firstborn of his flock and their fat. He did not labor as Cain did to bring this forth, but it was dear to him. Both brothers would have heard how their mother and father had attempted to cover their nakedness with fig leaves that represented their own works to cover their sin. But God demonstrated acceptable sacrifice by covering Adam and Eve with the skin of an innocent animal. Adam and Eve were ignorant of this unacceptable covering of their sin. But having been shown God's way they were no longer ignorant, nor were their children.

Cain had tried to win God's acceptance apart from His counsel. God responded by showing He would accept those who came to Him under His parameters of grace (Abel's sacrifice) and would reject what was attempted under the domain of the "knowledge of good and evil" (Cain's religious works). He then instructed Cain that if he would do good, he'd be accepted; but if he would not choose life, then sin would master him.

Cain was offended with the Lord. Rather than repent and do what was right, allowing this situation to strengthen his character, he vented on Abel his anger and offense with God. He murdered Abel. God said to Cain:

> So now you are cursed from the earth, which has opened its mouth to receive your brother's blood from your hand. When you till the ground, it shall *no longer yield its strength to you*. A *fugitive* and a *vagabond* you shall be on the earth.
>
> —GENESIS 4:11–12, EMPHASIS ADDED

The thing Cain feared most, to be rejected by God, he brought as a judgment on himself. The very medium through which he tried to win God's approval was now cursed by his own hand. The bloodshed now brought a curse. The ground would no longer give up its strength to him. Fruit would come only through great effort.

Offended Christians also cut off their own ability to produce fruit. Jesus compared the heart with soil in the parable of the sower. Just as Cain's fields were barren, the soil of an offended heart is barren, poisoned by bitterness. Offended people still may experience miracles, words of utterance, strong preaching, and healing in their lives. But these are gifts of the Spirit, not fruits. We will be judged according to fruit, not gifting. A gift is given. Fruit is cultivated.

Notice that God said Cain would become a fugitive and a vagabond as a result of his actions. There are numerous spiritual fugitives and vagabonds in our churches today. Their gifts of singing, preaching, prophesying, and so on are not received by the leadership in their previous church, so off they go. They are running aimlessly and carry an offense, looking for that perfect church that will receive their gift and heal their hurts.

They feel beat up and persecuted. They feel as if they are modern-day Jeremiahs. It is "just them and God," with everyone else out to get them. They become unteachable. They get what I call a persecution complex: "Everyone is out to get me." They comfort themselves that they are just a persecuted saint or prophet of God. They are suspicious of everyone. This is exactly what happened to Cain. Look what he says:

> I shall be a fugitive and a vagabond on the earth, and *it will happen that anyone who finds me will kill me.*
> —GENESIS 4:14, EMPHASIS ADDED

Consider that Cain had the persecution complex—everyone was out to get him! It is the same today. Offended people believe everyone is out to get them. With this attitude it is difficult for them to see areas in their own lives that need change. They isolate themselves and conduct themselves in such a manner that invites abuse.

A man who isolates himself seeks his own desire; he rages against all wise judgment.

—Proverbs 18:1

God never created us to live separately and independently of each other. He likes it when His children care for and nurture each other. He is frustrated when we sulk and feel sorry for ourselves, making everyone else responsible for our happiness. He wants us to be active members of the family. He wants us to get our life from Him. An isolated person seeks only his own desire, not God's. He receives no counsel and sets himself up for deception.

I am not talking about seasons in which God calls individuals apart to equip and refresh them. I'm describing those who have imprisoned themselves. They wander from church to church, relationship to relationship, and isolate themselves in their own world. They think that all who do not agree with them are wrong and are against them. They protect themselves in their isolation and feel safe in the controlled environment they have set up for themselves. They no longer have to confront their own character flaws. Rather than facing the difficulties, they try to escape the test. The character development that comes only as they work through conflicts with others is lost as the cycle of offense begins again.

ACQUIRING AN OFFENSE KEEPS YOU FROM SEEING YOUR OWN CHARACTER FLAWS BECAUSE BLAME IS DEFERRED TO ANOTHER.

As a couple, we held a lot of unforgiveness and hurts for many years. We got to the stage where we had very few friends, and I was feeling isolated and unloved even though I was faithfully attending an excellent church. Then I read your book *The Bait of Satan*, and everything changed. I came face-to-face with my offenses and unforgiveness, and with God's help, I was set free!

—C. G., BELFAST, IRELAND

CHAPTER 6

HIDING FROM REALITY

*[They are] always learning and never able
to come to the knowledge of the truth.*
—2 TIMOTHY 3:7

I'M OFTEN ASKED, "WHEN SHOULD I LEAVE A CHURCH OR MINISTRY team? How bad does it have to get?" I respond, "Who sent you to the church you presently attend?"

The majority of the time they answer, "God did."

"If God sent you," I reply, "do not leave until God releases you. If the Lord is silent, He is often saying, 'Don't change a thing. Do not leave. Stay where I have placed you!'"

When God does instruct you to leave, you will go out with peace, no matter what the condition of the ministry.

For ye shall go out with joy, and be led forth with peace.
—ISAIAH 55:12, KJV

Therefore, your departure will not be based on the actions or behavior of others but rather on the Spirit's leading. So leaving a ministry is not based on how bad things are.

To leave with an offended or critical spirit is not the plan of God. It is reacting rather than acting on His guidance. Romans 8:14 says, "For as many as are led by the Spirit of God, these are sons of God."

Notice it does not say, "For as many as react to difficult situations, these are sons of God."

Almost every time the word *son* is used in the New Testament, it comes from the two Greek words: *teknon* and *huios*. A good definition for the word *teknon* is "one who is a son by mere fact of birth."[1]

When my first son, Addison, was born, he was John Bevere's son by mere fact that he came from my wife and me. When he was in the nursery in the midst of all the other newborns, you could not recognize him as my son by personality. When friends and family came to visit, they could not pick him out except by the name tag above his crib. He did not possess anything that set him apart. Addison would be considered a *teknon* of John and Lisa Bevere.

We find *teknon* used in Romans 8:15–16. It says that because we have received the spirit of adoption, "the Spirit Himself bears witness with our spirit that we are children [*teknon*] of God." When a person receives Jesus Christ as Lord, he is a child of God by fact of the new birth experience. (See John 1:12.)

The other Greek word translated *sons* in the New Testament is *huios*. Many times it is used in the New Testament to describe "one who can be identified as a son because he displays the character or characteristics of his parents."[2]

As my son Addison grew he started looking and acting like his father. When Addison was six, Lisa and I took a trip and left him with my parents. My mother told my wife that Addison was almost a carbon copy of his daddy. His personality was like mine when I was his age. As he has grown, he has become more like his dad. He now can be recognized as John Bevere's son, not only by the fact of his birth but also by the characteristics and a personality that resemble his father's.

So, to put it simply, the Greek word *teknon* means "babies or immature sons," and the Greek word *huios* is most often used to describe "mature sons."[3]

Looking at Romans 8:14 again it reads: "For as many as are led by the Spirit of God, these are the sons [*huios*] of God." We can see clearly that it is the mature sons who are led by the Spirit of God. Immature Christians are less likely to follow the leading of the Spirit of God. Most often they react or respond emotionally or intellectually to circumstances they face. They have not yet learned to act only on the Spirit of God's leading.

As Addison grows, he will progress in character development. The more mature he becomes, the more responsibility I will entrust to him. It is wrong for him to stay immature. It is not God's will that we remain babies.

One way the character of my son Addison has grown is by facing difficult situations. When he started school he met up with some "bullies." I heard some of the things these rough kids were doing and saying to my son, and I wanted to go and deal with it. But I knew that would be wrong. For me to intervene would hinder Addison's growth.

So my wife and I continued to counsel him at home, preparing him to face the persecutions at school. He grew in character through obeying our counsel in the midst of his suffering.

This is similar to what God does with us. The Bible says, "Though He [Jesus] was a Son [*Huios*], yet He *learned obedience* by the things which He *suffered*" (Heb. 5:8, emphasis added).

Physical growth is a function of time. No two-year-old child has ever been six feet tall. Intellectual growth is a function of learning. Spiritual growth is a function of neither time nor learning, but it is a function of obedience. Now look at what Peter says:

> Therefore, since Christ suffered for us in the flesh, arm yourselves also with the same mind, for *he who has suffered in the flesh has ceased from sin.*
>
> —1 Peter 4:1, emphasis added

A person who has ceased from sin is a perfectly obedient child of God. He is mature. He chooses God's ways, not his own. Just as Jesus learned obedience by the things He suffered, we learn obedience by the difficult circumstances we face. When we obey the Word of God that is spoken by the Holy Spirit, we will grow and mature in the times of conflict and suffering. Our knowledge of Scripture is not the key. Obedience is.

Now we understand one reason why we have people in the church who have been Christians for twenty years, who can quote verses and chapters of the Bible, have heard a thousand sermons, and read many books, but still wear spiritual diapers. Every time they meet with difficult situations, rather than responding by the Spirit of God, they seek to protect themselves in their own way. They are "always learning and never able to come to the knowledge of the truth" (2 Tim. 3:7). They never come to the knowledge of the truth because they do not apply it.

Truth must be allowed to have its way in our lives if we are going to grow and mature. It is not enough to give mental assent to it without obeying it. Even though we continue to learn, we never mature because of disobedience.

SELF-PRESERVATION

A common excuse for self-preservation through disobedience is offense. There is a false sense of self-protection in harboring an offense. It keeps you from seeing your own character flaws because the blame is deferred to another. You never have to face your role, your immaturity, or your sin because you see only the faults of the offender. Therefore, God's attempt to develop character in you by this opposition is now abandoned. The offended person will avoid the source of the offense and eventually flee, becoming a spiritual vagabond.

Recently a woman told me about a friend of hers who left one church and began attending another. She invited the new pastor over for dinner. In the course of the conversation the pastor asked why she left the first church. The lady told him about all the problems in the leadership of her previous church.

The pastor listened and attempted to comfort her. From experience, I know it would have been wise for that pastor to encourage the woman by the Word of God to deal with her hurt and critical attitude. If necessary, he should have suggested that she return to her former church until God released her in peace.

When God releases you in peace, you will not have pressure to justify your departure to others. You will not be under pressure to judge or critically expose the problems your previous church had. I knew it would only be a matter of time before she would respond to this new pastor and his leadership in the same manner she had her previous one. When we retain an offense in our hearts, we filter everything through it.

There is an old parable that fits this situation. Back in the days when the settlers were moving to the West, a wise man stood on a hill outside a new Western town. As the settlers came from the East, the wise man was the first person they met before coming to the settlement. They asked eagerly what the people of the town were like.

He answered them with a question: "What were the people like in the town you just left?"

Some said, "The town we came from was wicked. The people were rude gossips who took advantage of innocent people. It was filled with thieves and liars."

The wise man answered, "This town is the same as the one you left."

They thanked the man for saving them from the trouble they had just come out of. They then moved on further west.

Then another group of settlers arrived and asked the same question: "What is this town like?"

The wise man asked again, "What was the town like where you came from?"

These responded, "It was wonderful! We had dear friends. Everyone looked out for the others' interest. There was never any lack because all cared for one another. If someone had a big project, the entire community gathered to help. It was a hard decision to leave, but we felt compelled to make way for future generations by going west as pioneers."

The wise old man said to them exactly what he had said to the other group: "This town is the same as the one you left."

These people responded with joy, "Let's settle here!"

How they viewed their past relations was their scope for their future ones.

The way you leave a church or a relationship is the way you will enter into your next church or relationship. Jesus said in John 20:23, "If you forgive the sins of any, they are forgiven them; if you retain the sins of any, they are retained."

We preserve the sins of other people when we pick up an offense and harbor resentment. If we leave a church or a relationship resentful and embittered, we will enter into the next church or relationship with that same attitude. It will then be easier to leave our next relationship when problems arise. We are dealing not only with the hurts that took place in the new relationship, but also with the hurts from our former relationship.

Statistics say 60 to 65 percent of divorced people end up getting divorced again after remarrying.[4] The manner in which a person leaves their first marriage determines the path into their second marriage. The unforgiveness they hold against their first mate hinders the future for their second one. In blaming the other they are blind to their own role or faulty characteristics. To make matters worse, now they have the added fear of being hurt.

This principle is not limited to marriage and divorce. It can apply to all relationships. A man who had previously worked for another minister came to work for our ministry team. He had been hurt by this former leader, but time had passed, and I felt the Lord was leading me to ask him to come work with us. I believed he was in the process of overcoming this hurt.

I called his former employer and shared my plans to bring him on staff. He encouraged me and thought it was a good move because he knew I cared for both of them. He believed the healing could be completed while he worked with us. I told both men that my prayer was for restoration and healing in their relationship.

When the man joined our ministry team, there were problems almost immediately. I'd address the issue only to see temporary relief. It seemed he couldn't get beyond his former relationship. It kept coming back to haunt him. He even accused me of doing the same things his previous leader had.

I was troubled because the well-being of this man was more important to me than what he could do for me as an employee. I made exceptions for him that I would not make for any other employee because I desired to see him healed.

After only two months he resigned. He felt trapped in the same situation as before. He left saying, "John, I will never work for another ministry again."

I blessed him and watched him go. We love him and his wife. The sad fact is that there is a strong call on his life for the very thing he has left, though that does not mean he won't have success in other areas.

I was troubled after he left so I sought the Lord. "Why did he leave so quickly when both of us felt so right about it?"

A few weeks later the Lord used a wise pastor friend of mine to answer this question. He said, "Many times God will allow people to run from situations He desires them to face if they are set on running from them in their hearts."

He then relayed the story of Elijah, who ran from Jezebel. (See 1 Kings 18–19.) Elijah had just executed the evil prophets of Baal and Asherah. They were the men who had led the nation into idolatry and had eaten at Jezebel's table. When Jezebel heard this, she threatened to kill Elijah within twenty-four hours.

God wanted Elijah to confront her, but instead he ran. He was so discouraged that he prayed to die. He was in no condition to fulfill the assignment. God sent an angel to feed him with two cakes and allowed him to run for forty days and nights to Mount Horeb.

When he arrived, the first thing God asked him was, "What are you doing here, Elijah?"

This seemed like a strange question. The Lord gave him the food for the journey, allowing him to go, only to ask him when he arrived, "What are you doing here?" God knew Elijah was set on escaping the difficult situation. So He allowed it, though it is obvious from His question that it wasn't His original plan.

He then said to Elijah, "Go, return on your way to the Wilderness of Damascus; and when you arrive, anoint...Jehu the son of Nimshi as king over Israel. And Elisha the son of Shaphat of Abel Meholah you shall anoint as prophet in your place" (1 Kings 19:15–16). Under Elisha's and Jehu's ministries this wicked queen and her evil system were destroyed (2 Kings 9–10). This assignment was not completed by Elijah but by the successors God told him to anoint in his place.

The pastor said to me, "If we are so set in our hearts not to face difficult situations, God will actually release us even though it is not His perfect will."

I later remembered an incident in Numbers 22 that illustrates this same point. Balaam wanted to curse Israel because there were great rewards in it for him personally.

He asked the Lord the first time if he could go, and God showed him that His will for Balaam was not to go. When the princes of Moab returned with more money and honor, Balaam went to God again. It is ridiculous to think God's mind would now change because more money and honor were in it for Balaam. But this time God said to go with them.

Now why did God change His mind? The answer is that God did *not* change His mind. Balaam was so set on going that God let him go. That is why His anger was aroused against Balaam when he did go.

We can pester the Lord regarding something for which He has already shown us His will. He will then allow us to do what we want even when it is against His original plan—even when it is not in our best interest.

Often God's plan causes us to face hurts and attitudes we don't want to face. Yet we run from the very thing that will bring strength to our lives. Refusing to deal with an offense will not free us from the problem. It will only give us temporary relief. The root of the problem remains untouched.

My experience with the young man that I hired also taught me a lesson about offenses and relationships. It is impossible to establish a healthy relationship with a person who has left another relationship bitter and offended. Healing must take place. Even though he kept saying he had forgiven his former leader, it was not forgotten.

Love forgets wrongs so that there is hope for the future. If we have truly overcome an offense, we earnestly seek to make peace. The time may not be right immediately, but in our hearts we will watch for an opportunity for restoration.

A wise friend said later, "There is an old proverb which states, 'Once a dog has been scalded with boiling water he will even fear cold water.'" How many today are afraid of the cold water that will bring refreshing because they have been burned once and cannot forgive?

Jesus desires to heal our wounds. But we often do not let Him heal them because it is not the easiest road to take. It is the path of humility and self-denial that leads to healing and spiritual maturity. It is the decision to make another's well-being more important than your own, even when that person has brought you great sorrow.

Pride cannot travel this path, but only those who desire peace at the risk of rejection. It is a trail that leads to humiliation and abasement. It is the road that leads to life.

WHAT WE LEARN IN THE PRESENCE OF GOD CANNOT BE LEARNED IN THE PRESENCE OF MEN.

I have been reading *The Bait of Satan*. My view of God's Word has been changed ever since. I'd gone through something that was very painful, and had it not been for the message of that book, I might have been trapped for eternity.

—F. N., MALAYSIA

CHAPTER 7

THE SURE FOUNDATION

Therefore thus says the Lord GOD: "Behold, I lay in Zion a stone for a foundation, a tried stone, a precious cornerstone, a sure foundation; whoever believes will not act hastily."
—ISAIAH 28:16

WHOEVER BELIEVES WILL NOT ACT HASTILY." A PERSON WHO acts hastily is an unstable person because his actions are not properly founded. This person is easily moved and swayed by the storms of persecutions and trials. For example, let's look at what happened with Simon Peter.

Jesus had entered the region of Caesarea Philippi and asked His disciples, "Who do men say that I, the Son of man, am?" (Matt. 16:13).

Several disciples enthusiastically shared the opinion of the crowds about who Jesus was. Jesus waited until they finished, then He looked at them and asked them point-blank, "But who do you say that I am?" (v. 15).

I'm sure there was a confused, fearful look on most of the disciples' faces as they pondered this, mouths half open and speechless. Suddenly the men who were so eager to speak, airing others' opinions, were silenced. Perhaps they had never seriously asked this question of themselves. Whatever the case, they now realized they had no answer.

Jesus did what He does so well. He located their hearts with a question. He brought them to a true realization of what they did and did not know. They were living off the speculations of others, rather than establishing in their own hearts who Jesus really was. They had not confronted themselves.

Simon, who was renamed Peter by Jesus, was the only one of the disciples who could answer. He blurted out, "You are the Christ, the Son of the living God" (Matt. 16:16).

Jesus then responded to Him by saying, "Blessed are you, Simon Bar-Jonah, for flesh and blood has not revealed this to you, but My Father who is in heaven" (v. 17).

Jesus was explaining to Simon Peter the source for this revelation. Simon Peter had not received this knowledge by hearing the opinions of others or by what he was taught, but God had revealed it to him.

Simon Peter was very hungry for the things of God. He asked the most questions. It was he who walked on water, while the other eleven watched. He was a man who would not settle for someone else's opinion! He wanted to hear directly from the mouth of God.

This revealed knowledge of Jesus did not come by his senses, but it was a gift, illuminated in his heart in response to his hunger. Many had seen and witnessed what Simon Peter saw and witnessed, but their hearts were not as hungry to know the will of God as was Peter's.

First John 2:27 says, "But the anointing which you have received from Him abides in you, and you do not need that anyone teach you; but as the same anointing teaches you concerning all things, and is true, and is not a lie, and just as it has taught you…"

This anointing was teaching Simon Peter. He heard what everyone else had to say, and then he looked inward to what God had revealed. Once you receive revealed knowledge from God, no one can sway you. When God reveals something to you, it doesn't matter what the whole world says. They cannot change your heart.

Jesus then said to Simon Peter and the rest of the disciples, "On this rock [of knowledge revealed by God] I will build My church, and the gates of [hell] shall not prevail against it" (Matt. 16:18). So we see clearly that there is a sure foundation in the revealed Word of God; in this case it was Peter's understanding that Jesus was the Son of God.

THE ILLUMINATED WORD

I have often told congregations and individuals when I am preaching to listen for God's voice within my voice. So often we are so busy taking notes that we only record everything that is said. This yields a mental understanding of the Scriptures and their interpretations—head knowledge.

When we possess solely a head knowledge, two things can happen: (1) we are easily susceptible to hype or emotionalism, or (2) we are bound by our intellect. But this is not the sure foundation on which Jesus builds His church. He said it would be founded on the revealed Word, not just memorized verses.

When we listen to an anointed minister speak or as we read a book, we should look for the words or phrases that explode in our spirits. This is the word God is revealing to us. It conveys light and spiritual understanding. As the psalmist said, "The entrance of Your word gives light; it gives understanding to the simple" (Ps. 119:130). It is the entrance of His Word into our hearts, not minds, that illuminates and clarifies.

Often a minister may be speaking on one subject, yet God is illuminating something totally different in my own heart. On the other hand, God may anoint the exact words of that minister, and they explode within me. Either way it is the revealed Word of God to me. This is what changes us from being simple (void of understanding) to being mature (filled with understanding). This illuminated Word in our hearts is the foundation Jesus said His church would be grounded on.

Jesus compared the unveiled Word of God to a rock. A rock speaks of stability and strength. We recall the parable of the two houses, with one built on rock and the other on sand. When adversity—such as persecution, tribulation, and affliction—stormed against both houses, the one built on sand was destroyed, while the house built on rock stood.

Some things we need to hear from God cannot be found in the Bible. For example, whom should we marry? Where should we work? What church should we join? And the list goes on. We must have the revealed Word of God for these decisions as well. Without it our decisions are founded on unstable ground.

What God reveals by His Spirit cannot be taken from us. This must be the foundation of all we do. Without it we will be easily offended by trials and tribulations that blindside us.

Again recall what Jesus said about the Word being heard and received with excitement yet not taking root in our hearts. It was received with gladness in the mind and emotions.

> Who, when they have heard the word, immediately receive it with gladness; and have *no root* in themselves, and so endure but for a time: afterward, when affliction or persecution ariseth for the word's sake, immediately they are *offended*.
> —MARK 4:16–17, KJV, EMPHASIS ADDED

We can easily interchange the words *root* and *foundation* for they both indicate the stabilizer and source of strength for a plant or structure. A person who is not stabilized or founded in the revealed Word of God is a prime candidate to be moved along by the storm of offense.

How many are just like the disciples Jesus confronted? They live on what they have heard others say or preach. The opinions and statements of others are taken as truth without seeking the counsel or witness of the Spirit. We can only live and proclaim what is revealed to us by God. This is what Jesus builds His church on.

I once had an unmarried secretary who was happily dating a young man who also worked for the church. They were growing closer day by day. Everyone could see this relationship was going to end up in marriage. They were already discussing it seriously.

One Sunday night the senior pastor called them out and said, "Thus saith the Lord, you two will be married."

The next morning my secretary walked into the office on clouds. She was so excited. She asked if I would marry them, and I said I would be honored to. I set up an appointment to meet with them for counseling.

But I was uneasy. When they came into my office, my spirit was troubled. I looked at my secretary and asked if she knew this young man was the one God had selected for her. She responded with an enthusiastic, definite yes.

I then looked at him and asked, "Do you believe it is the will of God for you to marry this girl?"

He looked at me with his mouth half open for a moment then dropped his head and shook it as if to say, "No, I am not sure."

I looked at them both and then spoke to the young man. "I will not marry you. I don't care who prophesied over you or what was said. I don't care how many have said, 'You two make a lovely couple.' If God has not revealed His will in your heart, you have no business going on with this marriage.

"If you marry without God's revealing this as His perfect will to you," I continued, "when storms come—and they will come—you will have questions: What if I had married another girl? Would I have had these problems? I should have made sure it was God's will. I feel trapped.

"Then your heart will grow weary, and you will not be able to fight against the adversity that blows against your marriage. You will be a double-minded man and unstable in all your ways."

I sent them off and said there would be no reason to meet again. He was relieved. She was very upset. For the next week it was very uncomfortable in our office. But I knew I had spoken the truth. This was a time of testing for her. If God had truly spoken to her that this man was her husband, she would have to trust the Lord to reveal it to him and stay free from offense with me as well as with God. I told her to back off and let him have room to hear from God. She did.

Three weeks passed, and they requested another meeting. I immediately felt a sense of joy. This time when they came into the office, he looked at me with a sparkle in his eyes and said, "I know beyond any doubt that this is the woman God has given me to marry!" They were married seven months later.

When you know God has put you in a relationship or a church, the enemy will have a much more difficult time getting you out. You are founded on the revealed Word of God and will work through the conflicts even when it looks impossible.

NO OTHER OPTION

The first five years of marriage for my wife and me were very tough. We had hurt each other so severely that it seemed impossible to salvage the loving relationship we once had.

Only one thing kept us together: We both knew God had ordained our marriage. Therefore we did not make divorce an option. Our only option was to believe He would heal and change us. We both committed ourselves to this process, no matter how painful.

When I had thoughts of giving up, I remembered the promises God had given me concerning our marriage. I was not ready to abort what God had designed and decreed for our union together.

One promise God had given us was that my wife and I would minister together. At the time He gave it, I thought, "I can easily see that. His hand is on us both for ministry."

In the midst of our marital storms, I could no longer see the promise clearly. But I refused to let go of it. Natural hope was gone because of strife and pride that had entered our marriage. Yet there was still a supernatural seed of life in my heart. That promise was an anchor or foundation in the time I needed it.

As it turned out, God not only healed our relationship but also made it much stronger than before. We grew from the conflicts by forgiving one another and learning from them. We now minister together. I consider my wife not only my lover and best friend but also the minister in whom I place the most confidence. I confide in her more than in any other person.

After coming through those rough first five years, I realized that God saw flaws in both of our lives—and our relationship brought them out into the light.

I was in awe of the wisdom of our being joined as man and wife. Before I met Lisa I prayed diligently for the woman I would one day marry. That choice was the second most important decision of my life—next to obeying the gospel. Because of praying and waiting on God's choice for my mate, I thought I would not have the problems others had in marriage. Oh, how wrong I was!

God selected a wife for me who was the desire of my heart. But she also exposed the selfish immaturity that was hidden in me. And there was much! To run from the conflict by choosing divorce or by blaming her would have only buried my immaturity under another layer of counterfeit protection called offense. Knowing the Word of God for marriage kept me from leaving.

At this point, I must detour from the main thrust of this chapter. Some of you who are reading this may be thinking, "I was not saved when I was married."

To you God says, "Now to the married I command, yet not I but the Lord: A wife is not to depart from her husband. But even if she does depart, let her remain unmarried or be reconciled to her husband. And a husband is not to divorce his wife....Brethren, let each one remain with God in that state in which he was called" (1 Cor. 7:10–11, 24).

Let this word on the covenant of marriage be settled in your heart so that you are not moved from your steadfastness by the trap of offense. Then seek the Lord for His revealed Word for your marriage.

Some of you may not have married in the will of God even as believers. To enter into the blessing of God for your marriage, you must repent of not seeking His counsel before marrying, and He will forgive you. Settle it in your heart that two wrongs do not make a right—to break a covenant because of offense is not the answer. Then seek the Lord for His Word for your marriage.

THE SOLID ROCK

The revealed Word of God is the solid rock on which we are to build our lives and ministries. Numerous people have told me of the many churches or ministry teams they have been a part of in only a short time. My heart grieves as I see how they are moved by trials and not by God's direction. They extol how wrong things are or how badly they and others were treated. They feel justified in their decisions. But their reasoning is only another layer of deception that keeps them from seeing the offense and their own character flaws.

They describe their present relation to the ministries or churches they are now part of as "temporary" or "this is where God has me for now." I even heard one man say, "I'm on loan to this church." They make these statements so that, if things get difficult, they have an escape route. They have no foundation to stand on in the new places they go; storms can blow them easily to the next port.

WHERE COULD WE GO?

To return to the example where Jesus asks His disciples who they say He is, we see the stability that comes when you know the revealed will of God. Look at Simon Peter.

After Simon told what the Father revealed to his heart, Jesus said, "And I also say to you that you are Peter, and on this rock I will build My church, and the gates of Hades shall not prevail against it" (Matt. 16:18).

Jesus changed Simon's name to Peter. This is significant for the name *Simon* means "to hear."[1] The name *Peter* (the Greek word being *petros)* means "a stone."[2] As a result of hearing the revealed Word of God in his heart he became a stone. A house built of stones on the solid foundation of a rock will endure the storms that beat against it.

The word *rock* in this verse comes from the Greek word *petra,* which means "a large rock."[3] Jesus was saying to Simon Peter that he was now made of the substance on which the house was to be founded.

Peter later wrote in 1 Peter 2:5, "You also, as living stones, are being built up a spiritual house." A stone is a small piece of a large rock. Strength, stability, and power are in the rock of the revealed Word of God, and there is fruit in the life of a person who receives it. That person is made strong with the strength of the one who is the living Word of God, Jesus Christ.

As the apostle Paul writes in 1 Corinthians 3:11, "For no other foundation can anyone lay than that which is laid, which is Jesus Christ." As we seek Him who is the living Word of God, He will be revealed, and we will be established.

In John 5:16 we find that during the last days of Jesus's walk on earth, life became more difficult for His ministry team. The religious leaders and the Jews were persecuting Jesus, seeking to kill Him. When things started looking up and the people wanted to take Him by force and make Him king, He refused and walked away. (See John 6:15.)

"Why did He do that?" His disciples wondered. "This was His opportunity, and ours." They were getting troubled. The storms were blowing hard.

"We have left our families and jobs to follow this man. We have a lot at stake. We believe He is the coming One. After all, John the Baptist declared it, and we heard Simon Peter say it in Caesarea Philippi. Those are two witnesses. But why does He keep irritating the existing leaders? Why is He digging His own grave? Why does He make such hard statements as 'O faithless and perverse generation, how long shall I be with you?' to us, His own disciples?"

The offense was beginning to mount in these men who had left all to follow Jesus.

Then the ultimate happened. Jesus preached something to them that sounded like flat-out heresy: "Most assuredly, I say to you, unless you eat the flesh of the Son of Man and drink His blood, you have no life in you" (John 6:53).

"What is He preaching now?" they wondered. "This is too far out for me!" Not only that, but He also said these things in front of the leaders in the synagogue in Capernaum. For these disciples this was the straw that broke the camel's back!

> Therefore many of His disciples, when they heard this, said, "This is a hard saying; who can understand it?"
>
> —JOHN 6:60

Notice the response of Jesus:

> When Jesus knew in Himself that His disciples complained about this, He said to them, "Does this offend you?"
>
> —JOHN 6:61

These are His own disciples! He does not retract the truth but instead confronts these men. He knows some have been living on a faulty foundation. He exposes that foundation and gives them an opportunity to see their own hearts. But they were not like Simon Peter or the other disciples who hungered for the truth. Look at their reaction:

> From that time many of His disciples went back and walked with Him no more.
>
> —JOHN 6:66, EMPHASIS ADDED

Notice it was not a few; it was "many." Some were no doubt the same ones who were so quick to say earlier in Caesarea Philippi, "Some say John the Baptist, some Elijah, and others Jeremiah or one of the prophets" (Matt. 16:14). They were not founded on the revealed Word of God.

The offense built to the point where they did what many do today—they left. They thought they had been deceived and mistreated, but they were not. They did not see truth because their eyes were focused on their own selfish desires.

Now look at what happens with Simon Peter as Jesus confronted the twelve:

> Then Jesus said to the twelve, "Do you also want to go away?" But Simon Peter answered Him, "Lord, to whom shall we go? You have the words of eternal life. Also we have come to believe and know that *You are the Christ, the Son of the living God.*"
> —JOHN 6:67–69, EMPHASIS ADDED

Jesus didn't beg these men, "Please don't leave. I just lost most of My staff. How would I get along without you!" No, He confronts them. "Do you also want to go away?"

Notice how Simon Peter answers, even though he is wrestling with the same opportunity to be offended as the others. "Lord, to whom shall we go?"

What he heard must have confused him, but there was a knowing in him that the others didn't possess. At Caesarea Philippi, Peter had a revelation of who Jesus really was: "the Son of the living God" (Matt. 16:16).

Now, in the heat of this trial, he spoke what was rooted in his heart: "We have come to believe and know that *You are the Christ, the Son of the living God.*" These are the exact words he blurted out in Caesarea Philippi. He was a stone, set on the established rock of the living Word of God. He would not leave offended.

REACTION UNDER PRESSURE

I often say that trials and tests *locate* a person. In other words, they determine where you are spiritually. They reveal the true condition of your heart. How you react under pressure is how the *real you* reacts.

You can have a house built on sand that is five stories high and beautiful, decorated with the most elaborate materials and craftsmanship. As long as the sun is shining, it looks like a bulwark of strength and beauty.

Next to that house you can have a single-story plain house. It is almost unnoticeable and possibly unattractive compared to the beautiful edifice next to it. But it is built on something you can't see—a rock.

As long as no storms strike, the five-story house looks much nicer. But when it encounters a severe storm, the five-story house collapses and is ruined. It may survive a few minor storms, but not the hurricane. The plain, one-story structure survives. The larger the house, the harder and more noteworthy its fall.

Some people in the church are like the disciples who were so quick to speak in Caesarea Philippi, but only later to be exposed. They may look like five-story Christians, the picture of strength, stability, and beauty. They may weather a few minor and midsize storms. But when a mighty storm blows in, they are relocated.

Be sure that you build your life on God's revealed Word, not what others say. Keep seeking the Lord and listening to your heart. Don't do or say things just because everyone else does. Seek Him and stand on what is illuminated in your heart!

WHEN THE
ENEMY SHAKES, IT IS
TO DESTROY. BUT GOD HAS A
DIFFERENT PURPOSE.

I would like to thank God for the message of *The Bait of Satan*. I have been fasting and praying for a breakthrough in my life. The Lord led me to this message, and it has radically changed my life. This is a must-read for all who are in leadership.

—C. P., NEW ZEALAND

CHAPTER 8

ALL THAT CAN BE SHAKEN
WILL BE SHAKEN

*He has promised, saying, "Yet once more I shake not
only the earth, but also heaven." Now this, "Yet once
more," indicates the removal of those things that
are being shaken, as of things that are made, that
the things which cannot be shaken may remain.*
—HEBREWS 12:26–27

IN THE PREVIOUS CHAPTER WE SAW THAT THE REVEALED WORD
of God is the foundation on which Jesus builds His church. We
watched Simon Peter remain even when other disciples left offended.
Even when Jesus gave him an opportunity to leave, Simon Peter spoke
what was established in his heart.

Now let's look at another test for Simon Peter—the night Jesus
was betrayed.

Jesus was seated with His twelve apostles, giving thanks and
serving Communion, when He made a startling statement: "Behold,
the hand of My betrayer is with Me on the table. And truly the Son
of Man goes as it has been determined, but woe to that man by whom
He is betrayed!" (Luke 22:21–22). What an announcement! We would
say today that Jesus had "dropped a bomb" with those words.

Although Jesus knew from the beginning that He would be betrayed, it was the first His disciples had heard of it. Can you imagine the horrible feeling in the room as He said that one of them who had been with Him from the start, a close associate, was going to betray Him?

In response, "they began to question among themselves, which of them it was who would do this thing" (v. 23). They were overwhelmed with shock that one of them would be capable of such a horrifying thing. But their motive for this investigation was not pure. We know this by how their conversation ended. Their reason for the inquest was selfish and full of pride. Look at the very next verse of Scripture:

> Now there was also a dispute among them, as to which of them should be considered the greatest.
>
> —LUKE 22:24

Picture this: Jesus told them He was about to be turned over to the chief priests to be condemned to death and delivered to the Romans to be mocked, scourged, and killed. The one who would do this was sitting with Him at the table.

The disciples questioned who it was, and it ended up in an argument about which of them would be the greatest. It was dishonorable—almost like children arguing over an inheritance. There was no concern for Jesus, but a jockeying for power and position. What unimaginable selfishness!

If I had been in Jesus' position, I might have asked if they had heard what I had said or if they even cared. We see from this incident an example of how the Master walked in love and patience. Most of us, if in Jesus's place, would have said, "Every one of you, get out! I am in My greatest hour of need, and you're thinking of yourselves!" What an opportunity to become offended!

We can almost guess who initiated the dispute among the disciples: Simon Peter, since he had the most dominating personality of the group and was usually the one who spoke up first.

He was probably quick to remind the others how he had been the only one to walk on water. Or perhaps he refreshed them about how he had had the first revelation of who Jesus really was. Then he may have shared again his experience on the Mount of Transfiguration with Jesus, Moses, and Elijah.

Peter was fairly confident that he was the greatest of the twelve. But this confidence was not rooted in love. Rather it was anchored in pride.

Jesus looked at all of them and told them they were acting as mere men, not sons of the kingdom: "The kings of the Gentiles exercise lordship over them, and those who exercise authority over them are called 'benefactors.' But not so among you; on the contrary, he who is greatest among you, let him be as the younger, and he who governs as he who serves. For who is greater, he who sits at the table, or he who serves? Is it not he who sits at the table? Yet I am among you as the One who serves" (Luke 22:25–27).

THE PURPOSE OF SIFTING

Even though Simon Peter had received abundant revelation of who Jesus was, he was not yet walking in the character and humility of Christ. He was building his life and ministry with past victories and pride. Paul admonished us in 1 Corinthians 3:10 to take heed how we build on our foundation in Christ.

Simon Peter was not building with the materials necessary for the kingdom of God but with supplies such as a strong will and personal confidence. Though unaware, he was still awaiting the transformation of his character. His reference was from the "pride of life" (1 John 2:16).

Pride would never be strong enough to equip him to fulfill his destiny in Christ. If not removed, this pride would eventually destroy him. In Ezekiel 28:11–19 we see that pride was the same character flaw found in Lucifer, God's anointed cherub, causing his downfall.

Now look at what Jesus says to Simon Peter:

And the Lord said, "Simon, Simon! Indeed, Satan has asked for you, that he may sift you as wheat."

—Luke 22:31

Pride opened the door for the enemy to come in and sift Simon Peter. The word *sift* is translated from the Greek word *siniazo*. It means "to sift, shake in a sieve; fig. by inward agitation to try one's faith to the verge of overthrow."[1]

Now if Jesus had had the mentality many have in the church, He would have said, "Let's pray, guys, and bind this attack of the devil. We are not going to let Satan do this to our beloved Simon!" But look at what He says:

> But I have prayed for you, that your faith should not fail; and when
> you have returned to Me, strengthen your brethren.
>
> —LUKE 22:32

Jesus did not pray that Simon Peter would escape this intense shaking to the point of overthrow. He prayed that his faith would not fail in the process. Jesus knew that out of this trial would emerge a new character, the one Simon Peter needed to fulfill his destiny and strengthen his brethren.

Satan had requested permission to shake Simon Peter so severely that he would lose his faith. The enemy's intent was to destroy this man of great potential, who had received so much revelation. But God had a different purpose for the shaking, and, as always, God is way ahead of the devil. He allowed the enemy to do this in order to shake everything in Simon Peter that *needed* to be shaken.

God showed my wife, Lisa, five purposes for shaking an object:

1. To bring it closer to its foundation
2. To remove what is dead
3. To harvest what is ripe
4. To awaken
5. To unify or mix together so it can no longer be separated

Any thought process or heart attitude that is rooted in selfishness or pride will be purged. As a result of this tremendous shaking, all of Simon Peter's self-confidence would be gone, and all that would remain was God's sure foundation. He would be awakened to his true condition, the dead would be removed and the ripe fruit harvested, bringing him closer to his true foundation. He would no longer function independently but would be interdependent on the Lord.

Peter boldly countered Jesus's words: "Lord, I am ready to go with You, both to prison and death." This statement was not born of the Spirit but out of his own self-confidence. He could not see the foreshadowing of this shaking.

JUDAS VERSUS SIMON

Some think Peter was a big talker and cowardly. But in the garden, when the temple guard came to arrest Jesus, Peter unsheathed his sword and struck the high priest's servant, cutting off his right ear (John 18:10). Not many cowards attack when they are outnumbered by enemy soldiers. So he was strong, but his strength was in his own personality, not in God's humility, for the sifting had not yet begun.

It happened just as Jesus predicted. The same bold, strong Simon Peter, ready to die for Jesus, wielding the sword in the garden full of soldiers, was confronted by a little servant girl. He was intimidated by her and denied even knowing Jesus.

Some think it is the big things that cause men to stumble. Often it is the minor ones that shake us the most. This shows the futility of self-confidence.

Then Peter denied Jesus two more times. Immediately the rooster crowed, and Peter left and wept bitterly. He was shaken of all his self-confidence and believed he could never rise again. All he had left, though he was not even aware of it, was what was revealed to him by the Spirit.

Simon Peter and Judas were similar in many ways, including the fact that they both rejected Jesus in the crucial last days of Jesus's life. Yet the two men had a fundamental difference.

Judas never longed to know Jesus in the manner that Simon did. Judas was not founded in Him. It appeared that he loved Jesus since he had left all to follow Him, traveled in His constant companionship, and even stayed under the heat of persecution. He cast out devils, healed the sick, and preached the gospel. (Recall that Jesus sent out the *twelve* to preach, heal, and deliver, not the eleven.) But his sacrifices were not out of love for Jesus or out of a revelation of who He was.

Judas had his own agenda from the start. He never repented of his self-seeking motives. His character was revealed by statements such as: "What are you willing *to give me* if I..." (Matt. 26:14, emphasis added). He lied and flattered to gain advantage (Matt. 26:25). He took money from the treasury of Jesus's ministry for personal use (John 12:4–6). And the list goes on. He never knew the Lord even though he spent three and a half years in His company.

Both men were sorry for what they had done. But Judas did not have the foundation Peter had. Because he never hungered to know Jesus, Jesus was not revealed to him. If Judas had a revelation of Jesus, he never could have betrayed Him. When a strong storm attacked his life, everything was shaken and blown away! See what happened:

> Then Judas, His betrayer, seeing that He had been condemned, was *remorseful* and brought back the thirty pieces of silver to the chief priests and elders, saying, "*I have sinned by betraying innocent blood.*" And they said, "What is that to us? You see to it!" Then he threw down the pieces of silver in the temple and departed, and went and *hanged himself.*
>
> —MATTHEW 27:3–5, EMPHASIS ADDED

He was remorseful and knew he had sinned. But he did not know the Christ. He had no understanding of the magnitude of whom he had betrayed. He only said, "I have betrayed innocent blood." If he had known the Christ as Simon Peter did, he would have gone back to Him and repented, knowing the goodness of the Lord. Committing suicide was yet another act of living independent of God's grace. The shaking revealed Judas had no foundation, even after following the Master for three years.

Numerous converts have prayed a "sinner's prayer," attended church, become active, and studied their Bibles. All of this, however, is without a revelation of who Jesus really is, though they confess Him with their mouths. When a severe disappointment occurs, they are offended with God and will have nothing to do with Him.

"God never did anything for me!" I've heard them say. "I tried Christianity, but my life only became more miserable." Or "I prayed and asked God to do this, and He did not do it!" They never laid their lives down for Jesus but tried to align themselves with Him for their own benefit. They served Him for what He could give them. They were easily offended. Here is Jesus' description of them:

Who, when they have heard the word, immediately receive it with gladness; and have *no root in themselves,* and so endure but for a time: afterward, when affliction or persecution ariseth for the word's sake, immediately they are *offended.*

—MARK 4:16–17, KJV, EMPHASIS ADDED

Notice that He said they were quickly offended because they had no foundation. In what are we to be rooted? We find the answer in Ephesians 3:16–18: We are to be rooted and grounded in love. Our love for God is our foundation.

Jesus said, "Greater love has no one than this, than to lay down one's life for his friends" (John 15:13). We cannot lay down our lives for someone we do not trust. We cannot lay down our lives for God unless we know Him well enough to trust Him. We must know and understand the nature and character of God. We must have the assurance that He would never do anything to harm us.

He always looks out for what He knows is in our best interest. What may look like a disappointment to us will always turn out for our good if we do not lose faith. God is love; there is no selfishness or evil in Him. It is Satan who desires to destroy us.

Often we view situations in our lives through short-range glasses. This distorts the true picture. God looks at the eternal aspect of what we go through. If we look at situations only from our limited vantage, two things can happen.

First, in the midst of God's purging process we will be easy prey to offense, whether it be with God or one of His servants. Second, we can easily be deceived by the enemy. Satan will use something that seems right at the moment, but his ultimate plan is to use that to our own destruction or death. When we are settled in trusting God, we are not moved from the Father's care. We will not succumb to the temptation to care for ourselves.

DEPENDING ON GOD'S CHARACTER

One way the enemy attempts to draw us away from trusting God is by perverting our perception of God's character. He did this in the garden with Eve when he asked her, "Has God indeed said, 'You shall *not* eat of *every tree* of the garden'?" (Gen. 3:1, emphasis added). He twisted God's commandment in order to attack and distort His character.

God had said, "Of *every tree* of the garden *you may freely eat;* but of the tree of the knowledge of good and evil you shall not eat, for in the day that you eat of it you shall surely die" (Gen. 2:16–17, emphasis added).

In essence the serpent was saying to Eve, "God is withholding everything good from you."

But God's emphasis was, "You may freely eat, except…" God had given mankind the entire garden to enjoy and all the fruit to eat with the exception of one.

The serpent was twisting how the woman saw God by saying, "God doesn't really care for you. What good thing is He keeping back from you? He must not love you as you thought. He must not be a good God!" She was deceived and believed a lie about God's character. The desire to sin was then aroused because God's Word was no longer life but law. And "the strength of sin is the law" (1 Cor. 15:56).

The enemy still operates this way today. He perverts the character of the Father God in His children's eyes. We have all had authorities over us such as dads, teachers, bosses, or governors who have been selfish and unloving. Because they are authority figures, it is easy to project their nature onto God's character since He is the ultimate authority.

The enemy has masterfully distorted the character of the Father by perverting our view of our earthly fathers. God says that, before Jesus returns, the hearts of the fathers will be returned to the children (Mal. 4:6). His character or nature will be seen in His leaders, and it will be a catalyst for healing.

When you know God would *never* do anything to harm or destroy you, and whatever He does or does not do in your life is in your best interest, then you will give yourself freely to Him. You will gladly be one to lay down your life for the Master.

If you have given yourself totally to Jesus and are committed to His care, you cannot be offended because you are not your own. Those who are hurt and disappointed are those who have come to Jesus for what He can do for them, not because of who He is.

When we have that attitude we are easily disappointed. Self-centeredness causes us to be shortsighted. We are unable to view our immediate circumstances through the eyes of faith. When our lives are truly lost in Jesus, we know His character and share His joy. We cannot be shaken or shipwrecked.

It is easy to become offended when we judge by our natural surroundings and circumstances. This is not seeing through the eyes of the Spirit. Often God does not answer me in the manner or amount of time I feel is absolutely necessary. But as I look back at every case I understand and can see His wisdom.

Occasionally our children do not understand our methods or the logic behind their training. We try to give explanations to the older children so they can benefit from the wisdom. But at times they may not understand or agree because of their immaturity; later on in life they will. Or perhaps the reason is to test their obedience, love, and maturity. It is the same with our Father in heaven. In these situations faith says, "I trust You even though I don't understand."

In Hebrews 11:35–39 we find the record of those who never saw the fulfillment of their promises from God and still never wavered: "Others were tortured, not accepting deliverance, that they might obtain a better resurrection. Still others had trial of mockings and scourgings, yes, and of chains and imprisonment. They were stoned, they were sawn in two, were tempted, were slain with the sword. They wandered about in sheepskins and goatskins, being destitute, afflicted, tormented—of whom the world was not worthy. They wandered in deserts and mountains, in dens and caves of the earth. And all these, having obtained a good testimony through faith, *did not receive the promise*" (emphasis added).

They had decided God was all they wanted, no matter what the cost. They believed Him even when they died without seeing the promises fulfilled. They could not be offended!

We are rooted and grounded when we bear this intense love and trust in God. No storm, no matter how intense, can ever move us. This does not come by strong will or personality. It is a gift of grace to all who place their confidence in God, throwing away the confidence of self. But to give yourself in total abandonment you must know the One who holds your life.

GRACE IS GIVEN TO THE HUMBLE

Simon Peter could no longer boast of being great. He had lost his natural confidence. He saw all too clearly the futility of his own strong will. He had been humbled. He was now a perfect candidate for the grace of God. God gives His grace to the humble. Humility is a prerequisite. It was a lesson burned in the conscience of Peter as he wrote in his epistle: "Be clothed with humility, for 'God resists the proud, but gives grace to the humble'" (1 Pet. 5:5).

Peter had been shaken to the verge of giving up. We know this by the message the angel of the Lord gave to Mary Magdalene at the tomb: "But go, tell His disciples—*and Peter*—that He is going before you into Galilee; there you will see Him, as He said to you" (Mark 16:7, emphasis added). The angel had to single him out. Peter was at the point of shipwreck, but God still had laid a foundation in him. It would not be removed by the shaking, but strengthened.

Jesus not only forgave Peter, but He also restored him. Now that he had been shaken, he was ready to become one of the central figures in the church. He courageously proclaimed the resurrection of Christ before the very ones responsible for His crucifixion. He faced the council, not a servant girl. With great authority and boldness he stood up to them.

History reports that Peter was crucified upside down after many years of faithful service.[2] He insisted he was unworthy to die the same death his Lord had died, so they hung him upside down. He was no longer afraid. He was a stone built on a solid foundation of the Rock.

Trials in this life will expose what is in your heart—whether the offense is toward God or others. Tests either make you bitter toward God and your peers or stronger. If you pass the test, your roots will shoot down deeper, stabilizing you and your future. If you fail, you become offended, which can lead to defilement with bitterness.

LORD, I HAVE SERVED YOU, SO WHY...?

When I was a pastor, a sharp, fourteen-year-old young man who was well respected by his friends and leaders was in the youth group. He was a good student and an accomplished athlete. Zealous for the things of God, the young man served faithfully and volunteered for every project. He took a missions trip with us, witnessing to almost everyone he met.

At one point in his life, he spent four hours a day in prayer. He heard many things from the Lord and shared them with others. What he shared was always a blessing. He acknowledged his call to the ministry and wanted to be a pastor before the age of twenty. He seemed to be an unshakable rock.

I loved this young man, recognized the call of God on his life, and invested my time in him. I had only one concern: He seemed to have too much confidence in himself. I wanted to say something to him but did not have a release to do so. I knew a change would come. He weathered some tough storms and yet stayed strong. Sometimes I questioned my discernment as I saw him endure severe trials.

A few years passed. He moved, and I began to travel full-time. But I kept in touch with him. I knew he would go through a breaking process. Since it had to take place, I had no idea what would happen but realized it was necessary for him in order to fulfill his destiny. This would be a similar process to Simon Peter's sifting.

When this young man was eighteen, his father contracted incurable cancer. The young man and his mother fasted and prayed, believing that his dad would be healed. Others joined with them as well. Only months earlier his dad had committed his life to the lordship of Jesus.

The father's condition grew worse. I was ministering in another city in Alabama when my wife called, urging me to telephone this young man. I reached him and could see he needed someone to encourage him.

I drove all that night after my last service, arriving at his house at four in the morning. His father's condition was so severe that the doctors gave him only days to live. He could not even communicate.

The young man was confident that his dad would rise up healed. I ministered to the family and left several hours later. The next morning we had a call saying things had taken a turn for the worse.

Lisa and I prayed immediately. As we did, God gave my wife a vision of Jesus standing by this man's bedside ready to take him home. Thirty minutes later the young man called and told us his father had passed away. He seemed to be his same strong self. But that was only the beginning.

That night he called some of his close friends to tell them his father had died. When they answered the phone, they were crying. He wondered how they had already heard the news. But they hadn't heard. The tears they were crying were for one of his best friends who had just been killed in an accident. In one day he had lost his father and a very good friend.

The shaking had begun. He was bewildered, frustrated, and numb. The presence of God seemed to have eluded him.

A month later, driving home, the young man came upon an accident that had just taken place. He had had emergency medical training and stopped. Everyone in both cars was a close friend of his. Two died in his arms while he was trying to help.

My young friend had reached his limit. He spent three hours in the woods praying and crying out to God. "Where are You? You said You would be my Comforter, and I have no comfort!"

It seemed as if God had turned His back on him. But this was, in fact, the first time his own strength had failed him.

He became angry with God. Why had He allowed this? He was not angry with his pastor, his family, or me. His offense was with God. He was consumed with frustration. God had failed him in his hour of greatest need.

"Lord, I've served You and laid many things down to follow You," he prayed. "Now You have abandoned me!" He believed God owed him something for all he had given up to serve Him.

Many people have experienced hurts and disappointments that are less extreme and some that are more. Many become offended with the Lord. They believe He should take into consideration all they have done for Him.

They are serving Him for the wrong reasons. We should not serve the Lord for what He can do but rather for who He is and what He has already done for us. Those who become offended do not fully realize how great a debt He has already paid for them to be free. They have forgotten from what manner of death they were delivered. They see through natural eyes rather than eternal.

This young man stopped going to church and started running around with the wrong crowd, frequenting bars and parties. In his frustration he wanted nothing to do with the things of the Lord. He wanted to avoid any contact with God.

He could not keep up this lifestyle for longer than two weeks, for his heart was deeply convicted. But he still refused to approach the Lord for six months. Even then the heavens seemed to be as brass. The presence of the Lord seemed nowhere to be found.

Over a year had gone by. Through several incidents he saw that God was still at work in his life. He approached God, but now it was different. He came humbly. After this time of trial was over, the Lord showed him how He had never left him. As his spiritual walk was restored, he learned to put his confidence in God's grace, not in his own strength.

I kept in touch with him. A year and a half later he told me things he had seen in himself that he never knew were there. "I was a man without character and shallow in all my relationships. I was raised by my dad to be strong outwardly, a self-made man. I could never have grown the way God wanted me to. I am thankful the Lord did not leave me in that condition.

"But what grieved my heart the most was not running around in bars and drinking. It was that I turned my back on the Holy Spirit. I love Him so much. My fellowship with Him has never been as sweet as it is now."

A lot of shaking occurred in his life. Self-confidence was eliminated. But this young man had the foundation that Simon Peter had, and it could not be taken away. Instead of building his life and ministry through pride, he is building by the grace of God.

Offenses will reveal the weakness and breaking points in our lives. Often the point where we think we are strong is our place of hidden weakness. It will remain hidden until a powerful storm blows away the cover. The apostle Paul wrote, "For we are the circumcision, who worship God in the Spirit, rejoice in Christ Jesus, and *have no confidence in the flesh*" (Phil. 3:3, emphasis added).

We can do nothing of eternal value in our own ability. It is easy to say this, but having this truth deeply rooted in our being is another matter.

JESUS DID NOT COMPROMISE TRUTH IN ORDER TO KEEP PEOPLE FROM BEING OFFENDED.

Your book *The Bait of Satan* really opened my eyes. My husband and I work in the ministry, and I was under the impression that I was all right with the Lord. *The Bait of Satan* showed me that the fifteen-year grudge I had been holding against my aunt would have cost me everything. We're always taught as Christians to forgive, but I never took it to heart until your message made me face that particular hurt in my past.

—R. M., TENNESSEE

CHAPTER 9

THE ROCK OF OFFENSE

"Behold, I lay in Zion a chief cornerstone, elect, precious,
and he who believes on Him will by no means be put to
shame." Therefore, to you who believe, He is precious; but
to those who are disobedient, "The stone which the builders
rejected has become the chief cornerstone," and "a stone
of stumbling and a rock of offense." They stumble, being
disobedient to the word, to which they also were appointed.
—I PETER 2:6–8

TODAY THE MEANING OF THE WORD *BELIEVE* HAS BEEN WEAKENED. In the eyes of most it has become a mere acknowledgment of a certain fact. To many it has nothing to do with obedience. But in the passage above, the words *believe* and *disobedient* are represented as opposites.

The Scriptures exhort "that whoever believes in Him [Jesus Christ] should not perish but have eternal life" (John 3:16). As a result of the way we view the word *believe*, many think that all they are required to do is believe that Jesus existed and died on Calvary, and they are in good standing with God. If this were the only requirement, the demons would be in good standing with Him. The Scriptures also say, "You believe that there is one God. You do well. *Even the demons believe*—and tremble" (James 2:19, emphasis added). Yet, there is no salvation for them.

The word *believe* has more meaning in the Scriptures than acknowledging existence of or just mentally assenting to a fact. Remaining true to the context of the verse above, we can say that the main element of believing is obedience. We could read it this way: "Therefore, to you who *obey,* He is precious; but to those who are *disobedient,* 'The stone which the builders rejected has become the chief cornerstone,' and *'a stone of stumbling and a rock of offense.'*"

It is not difficult to obey when you know the character and love of the one to whom you are submitting. Love is the bottom line in our relationship with the Lord—not love of principles or teachings but love for the Person of Jesus Christ. If that love is not firmly in place, we are susceptible to offense and stumbling.

The Israelites, whom the Lord called to be builders, rejected God's chief cornerstone, Jesus. They loved their teachings of the Old Testament. They were satisfied with their interpretations because they could be wielded to their own benefit and used to control others. Jesus, on the other hand, challenged all the legalism they held so dear. He pleaded with them, "You search the Scriptures, for in them you think you have eternal life; and these are they which testify of Me" (John 5:39).

They couldn't fathom the idea that from the beginning God desired sons and daughters with whom He could have a relationship. They wanted to rule and reign. The law had risen above relationship in their eyes. They rejected what was freely given to them. They would rather have earned it. So the free gift of God, Jesus Christ, their hope of life and salvation, became "a stone of stumbling and a rock of offense" to them.

Simeon prophesied as he lifted the baby Jesus in his arms in the temple: "Behold, this Child is destined for the fall and rising of many in Israel" (Luke 2:34). Notice the fall and rising. The One who was given to bring peace to the world ended up bringing a sword of division to the ones to whom He was sent (Matt. 10:34) and life to those who were victimized by the builders (the ministers of that day).

JESUS AND OFFENSES

In Sunday school Jesus was often presented as the shepherd carrying the lost lamb on His shoulders back to the fold. Or perhaps He had

His arms around the little children while blessing them or was smiling and saying, "I love you." These accounts are all true, but they do not give the whole picture.

This same Jesus also denounced the Pharisees for their self-righteousness: "Serpents, brood of vipers! How can you escape the condemnation of hell?" (Matt. 23:33). He turned over the tables of the moneychangers in the temple and ran them out (John 2:13–22). He told the man who wanted to bury his father before following Him, "Let the dead bury their own dead, but you go and preach the kingdom of God" (Luke 9:59–60). That isn't the end of the list either.

A close look at the ministry of Jesus reveals a Man who offended many while He ministered. Let's look at a few examples.

Jesus offended the Pharisees.

On many occasions Jesus confronted and offended these leaders. Because they were offended, they sent Him to the cross. They hated Him.

But Jesus loved them enough to speak the truth: "Hypocrites! Well did Isaiah prophesy about you, saying: 'These people draw near to Me with their mouth, and honor Me with their lips, but their heart is far from Me. And in vain they worship Me'" (Matt. 15:7–9). This statement offended them.

Notice what Jesus's disciples asked Him immediately afterward:

> Then His disciples came and said to Him, "Do You know that the Pharisees were *offended* when they heard this saying?"
> —MATTHEW 15:12, EMPHASIS ADDED

Study His response:

> Every plant which My heavenly Father has not planted will be uprooted. Let them alone. They are blind leaders of the blind. And if the blind leads the blind, both will fall into a ditch.
> —MATTHEW 15:13–14

Jesus showed that offenses will actually purge those who are not truly planted by His Father. Some people may join churches or ministry teams but have not been sent by God or are not of God. The offense that comes when truth is preached reveals their true motives and causes them to uproot themselves.

In visiting other churches I have witnessed many cases in which pastors grieve over people who have left, whether from the staff or the congregation. In most instances those people were upset because truth was preached, and it confronted their lifestyles. They would then become critical of every aspect of the church and leave.

For pastors to hold on to everyone who comes through their doors, they will eventually have to compromise truth. "If you preach the truth," I tell them, "you will offend people, and they will be uprooted and leave. Do not grieve over them, but rather continue to feed and nurture the ones God has sent you."

Some leaders avoid confrontation, afraid of losing people. Some are especially hesitant because those who need confronting are the big givers or influential in the church or community. Others are afraid of hurting the feelings of someone who may have been with them a long time. As a result the pastors lose the God-given authority to protect and feed the sheep entrusted to them.

When I first entered a pastoral position, a wise man warned me: "Stay in your authority, or someone else will take it from you and use it against you."

Samuel was a man of God who would not compromise truth for anyone, not even the king. When Saul disobeyed God, the Lord told Samuel to confront him. He did. Unfortunately, Saul did not respond to the word of the Lord with true repentance. He was more concerned about how he looked to other people. When Samuel started to leave him, Saul clutched at his robe and tore off a corner of it. Samuel devastated him with these words: "The LORD has torn the kingdom of Israel from you today" (1 Sam. 15:28).

This was not what Samuel wanted for Saul. He was grieved for him. He had anointed Saul as king, trained him to govern, and conducted his coronation. He was Saul's personal friend. But listen to how God reacted to Samuel's grief over Saul: "How long will you mourn for Saul, seeing *I have rejected him* from reigning over Israel? *Fill your horn with oil,* and go, I am sending you" (1 Sam. 16:1, emphasis added).

God was saying that in order for Samuel to continue to move in fresh oil or anointing, he had to realize God's love and judgment are perfect. If Samuel went back to Saul once God had rejected him, he wouldn't have had fresh oil. If he kept mourning, he would go nowhere.

Pastors who grieve and mourn over people who leave the church or who refuse to confront members because they are friends end up with the anointing oil in their lives running dry. Some ministries die, while others simply imitate being alive. Unknowingly they have chosen their relationship with men over their relationship with God.

The Bible does not record that Jesus reacted to any of the men who left Him. His only delight was to do the will of the Father. In doing so He would benefit the greatest number of people.

I will never forget the time I was preaching in a Spirit-filled denominational church. We had been on the road for about a year. The first Sunday morning I preached a simple message of repentance and returning to one's first love. I sensed the resistance but knew it was the message I was to bring.

After the service the pastor said, "God has shown me what you preached this morning, but I didn't think my people were ready for it."

My wife felt impressed by the Holy Spirit to ask him, "Who is the pastor of the church—you or Jesus?"

The pastor dropped his head. "That is exactly what the Lord said to me about a month ago. He told me that He knew what these people could handle." He told us that a third of his church was made up of "old liners" who did not want any change in the order of service, the music, or the preaching. We encouraged him to be strong and obey the Lord.

We did four more services in the church; each one was more difficult. When we left the city, I felt as if a sack of sand were in my gut. I couldn't figure it out. It got heavier and more unpleasant. Usually when I leave a church, joy fills my heart. I didn't know what was wrong.

When I finally got alone with the Lord, I asked, "Father, what did I do wrong? Why do I have this heavy burden in my spirit? Did I usurp the pastor's authority?"

He simply said, "Dust the dust off the bottom of your feet." (See Luke 9:5.)

I was shocked to hear Him say that. I kept praying and questioning Him, only to hear the same words: "Dust the dust off the bottom of your feet."

Finally I obeyed. As my hand left the sole of my second shoe, the heaviness lifted, and joy entered my heart. Again I said in amazement, "Lord, they did not attack me and throw me out of town. Why?"

He showed me that the leadership and many of the people had rejected His word to them.

"Give them more time, Lord," I petitioned.

"If I gave them fifty more years, they would not change. They have set their hearts."

I knew this leader had chosen to keep peace through compromise rather than obey God. His horn was not filled with fresh oil. He had the form without the substance. In other words, he had the appearance of being Spirit-filled yet lacked the power or presence of God. I later heard that he resigned as the pastor, and the church is just a fraction of what it was.

Jesus would not be controlled by others. He would speak truth even if it meant confrontation and ultimately offense. If you desire the approval of men, God's anointing cannot fall upon you. You must purpose in your heart to speak the Word of God and perform His will even at the risk of offending others.

Jesus offended those of His own hometown.

Jesus had come to His own hometown to minister. But He was unable to bring them the liberty and healing He had brought to so many others. Look at what they said:

> "Is this not the carpenter's son? Is not His mother called Mary? And His brothers James, Joses, Simon, and Judas? And His sisters, are they not all with us? Where then did this Man get all these things?" So they were *offended* at Him. But Jesus said to them, "A prophet is not without honor except in his own country and in his own house."
>
> —MATTHEW 13:55–57, EMPHASIS ADDED

Can you hear these men and women of Nazareth saying, "Who does He think He is, teaching us with authority? We know who He is. He grew up here. We are His elders. He is but a carpenter's son. He has had no formal training."

Again Jesus did not compromise truth in order to keep them from being offended. The townspeople were so angry that they tried to kill Him by pushing Him off a cliff (Luke 4:28–30). Even when His life was in danger He continued to speak the truth. How we need more men and women like that today!

Jesus offended His own family members.

Even those of His own house were offended by Him. They were not pleased with the pressure that was being put on them by what He was doing. They found it hard to believe He was behaving the way He was. Let's look:

> But when His own people [or "family," NIV] heard about this, they went out to lay hold of Him, for they said, "He is out of His mind." …His brothers and His mother came, and standing outside they sent to Him, calling Him. And a multitude was sitting around Him; and they said to Him, "Look, Your mother and Your brothers are outside seeking You." But He answered them, saying, "Who is My mother, or My brothers?" And He looked around in a circle at those who sat about Him, and said, "Here are My mother and My brothers! For whoever does the will of God is My brother and My sister and mother."
>
> —MARK 3:21, 31–35

His own family thought that He was out of His mind. Notice that the Scriptures say Jesus's family went out to take Him into custody. Mark identifies those relatives as Jesus's own mother and brothers who later found Him preaching in someone's house. Even John's Gospel says, "His brothers did not believe Him" (John 7:5).

Many have not realized that Jesus was rejected by those who were close to Him. But it was not the acceptance of His household He was looking for. He would not be controlled by their desires. He would fulfill the Father's plan whether they approved or not.

I have seen many, especially married couples, who have not followed Jesus for fear of offending their mates or family members. As a result they backslide or never reach the full potential of their calling.

When I was first born again, all the members of my family were Roman Catholics and did not share the excitement of my newly found faith. My mother in particular was very displeased with my decision to leave the church in which she brought me up. There are certainly precious Catholics who love God, but I knew God was calling me out.

A second blow came when I announced my decision to enter the ministry. I had just received my mechanical engineering degree from Purdue University, and my parents had high hopes for me. I knew what the Lord desired of me, and I knew it would offend those close to me. For years it was uncomfortable. There were a lot of misunderstandings. But I had decided that no matter how angry they might become, I would follow Jesus.

In the beginning I tried to run them over with the gospel. I told them they were not saved just by attending mass. I pushed them to their limits. I was not wise. Then God instructed me to live the Christian life before them and let them see my good works. I still did not compromise to please them.

Today my parents are very supportive, and my grandfather, who fought me the most, was gloriously saved at the age of eighty-nine, two years before his death.

Jesus's mother and brothers may have thought He had lost His mind. But because of His obedience to the Father, they all ended up saved and in the upper room on the Day of Pentecost. James, His half brother, became the leading apostle of the church in Jerusalem.

If we compromise what God tells us in order to please our family members, we will lose the fresh oil in our lives, and we will hinder them from being set free.

Jesus offended His own staff.

In a previous chapter we discussed in detail the viewpoint of the disciples when Jesus offended them. Let's review it again and see it from Jesus's perspective.

> Therefore many of His disciples, when they heard this, said, "This is a hard saying; who can understand it?" When Jesus knew in Himself that His disciples complained about this, He said to them, *"Does this offend you?"*…From that time many of His disciples went back and walked with Him no more.

Things were already tough enough as it was. The religious leaders were plotting His death. His own hometown rejected Him. His family thought He was out of His mind. To add more pressure, many of His own staff members left offended. But Jesus still did not compromise. He just told those who were left that they were also free to go if they wanted to.

The only thing that mattered to Jesus was fulfilling the Father's plan. If He had been left standing alone that day, it would not have changed His heart. He was determined to obey His Father.

Jesus offended some of His closest friends.

> Now a certain man was sick, Lazarus of Bethany, the town of Mary and her sister Martha. It was that Mary who anointed the Lord with fragrant oil and wiped His feet with her hair, whose brother Lazarus was sick. Therefore the sisters sent to Him, saying, "Lord, behold, he whom You love is sick."
>
> —JOHN 11:1–3

Jesus loved Martha, Mary, and Lazarus. They were close. He spent time with them. Notice His response when the news arrived that Lazarus was sick:

> So, when He heard that he was sick, He stayed two more days in the place where He was.
>
> —JOHN 11:6

Jesus knew by revelation that Lazarus's sickness would lead to death. It was a very serious matter. But He stayed where He was for two additional days. When He finally came to Bethany, Lazarus was already dead.

Martha and Mary each said to Him, "Lord, if You had been here, my brother would not have died" (John 11:21, 32). In other words, "Why didn't You come immediately? You could have saved him!"

Most likely both sisters were a little offended. They sent a messenger to tell Him, and He delayed for two days. Jesus did not respond as they expected. He didn't drop everything; instead He followed the leading of the Holy Spirit. This was best for everyone. However, at the time it looked as if Jesus was apathetic, as if He didn't care.

So often ministers are controlled by their people. They think they have to do everything the people ask of them.

A board member at a Spirit-filled church that had lost its pastor once told me, "We want a pastor who will meet our needs, one who can just come to my place at eight o'clock in the morning and have coffee."

I thought, "You will find a social man that you can control, not one controlled by the Holy Ghost." I found out later that this church had gone through four pastors in a year and a half.

When I was a youth pastor, a young man came to me after I had been pastoring for six months. "Will you be my buddy?" he asked. "My last youth pastor was my buddy."

The youth pastor before me was very sociable with the young people. They majored on activities. I knew what he was asking for. It was basically what the board member had wanted from his pastor.

I quoted Matthew 10:41 to him where Jesus said, "He who receives a prophet in the name of a prophet shall receive a prophet's reward. And he who receives a righteous man in the name of a righteous man shall receive a righteous man's reward."

"You have a lot of buddies, don't you?" I asked him.

"Yes," he answered.

"But you have only one youth pastor, don't you?"

"Yes."

"Do you want a youth pastor's reward or a buddy's reward? Because the way you receive me determines what you will receive from God."

He saw my point. "I want a youth pastor's reward."

Many ministers are afraid that if they do not fulfill their people's expectations they will hurt their feelings and lose their support. They are trapped by the fear of offending others. They are controlled by their own people, not God. As a result, little of eternal value is accomplished in their churches or congregations.

Jesus offended John the Baptist.

Even John the Baptist had to deal with the temptation of being offended with Jesus.

Then the disciples of John reported to him concerning all these things. And John, calling two of his disciples to him, sent them to Jesus, saying, "Are You the Coming One, or do we look for another?" When the men had come to Him, they said, "John the Baptist has sent us to You, saying, 'Are You the Coming One, or do we look for another?'"

—LUKE 7:18–20

Wait a minute. Why does John ask Jesus if He is the Coming One, the Messiah? John was the one who prepared His way and announced His arrival: "Behold! The Lamb of God who takes away the sin of the world!" (John 1:29). He was the one who said, "This is He who baptizes with the Holy Spirit" (v. 33). He even said, "He must increase, but I must decrease" (John 3:30). John was the only person who really knew who Jesus was at that time. (It had not yet been revealed to Simon Peter.)

Why is he asking, "Is Jesus the Messiah, or do we look for another?"

Put yourself in John's place. You have been the man on the cutting edge of what God is doing. Multitudes upon multitudes of people have received ministry from you. You have the most talked about outreach ministry in the nation. You have lived a life of self-denial. You have not even married in order to maximize the full potential of your call. You have lived in the desert eating locusts and wild honey and fasted often. You have fought the Pharisees and been accused of demon possession. Your whole life is spent preparing the way for this coming Messiah.

Now you're in prison. You have been locked up for quite some time. Very few people are coming to visit you because the attention of the people you prepared is now turned to Jesus of Nazareth. Even your own disciples have joined this Man. Only a few are left to serve you. When they come to see you, they bring stories of how this Man and His disciples live a very different life from yours. They eat and drink with tax collectors and sinners. They break the Sabbath and don't even fast.

You say to yourself, "I saw the Spirit descend as a dove on Him, but is this the behavior of a Messiah?"

The temptation to become offended grows greater the longer you're in prison. "This Man for whom I have spent my life preparing the way has not even come and visited me in jail! How can this be? If He is the Messiah, why doesn't He get me out of this prison? I've done no wrong."

So you send two of your faithful disciples to question Jesus. "Are You the coming One, or do we look for another?"

Let's look at Jesus's response to John:

And that very hour He cured many of infirmities, afflictions, and evil spirits; and to many blind He gave sight. Jesus answered and said to them, "Go and tell John the things you have seen and heard: that the blind see, the lame walk, the lepers are cleansed, the deaf hear, the dead are raised, the poor have the gospel preached to them. *And blessed is he who is not offended because of Me."*
—LUKE 7:21–23, EMPHASIS ADDED

The response of Jesus is prophetic. He quotes Isaiah, a book very familiar to John. The passages in Isaiah 29:18, 35:4–6, and 61:1 apply to all that John's disciples had observed while they waited to question Jesus. They bore witness of Him as Messiah. But He does not end it there. He adds, "And blessed is he who is not offended because of Me."

He was saying, "John, I know you don't understand all that is happening with you and many of My ways, but do not be offended with Me because I do not operate as you expected." He was urging John not to judge by his own understanding of God's ways in the past and in his own life and ministry. John didn't know the whole picture or plan of God, just as we do not know the complete picture today. Jesus was encouraging him, saying, "You've done what was commanded of you. Your reward will be great. Just stay free from offense with Me!"

OFFENSE WITHOUT APOLOGY

Even if you are trained in many of God's ways, as John was, you are still likely to have an opportunity to be offended with Jesus. If you truly love and believe on Him, you will fight to stay free from offense, realizing His ways are always higher than yours.

Also, if you are going to obey the Spirit of God, people will be offended by you. Jesus said in John 3:8, "The wind blows where it wishes, and you hear the sound of it, but cannot tell where it comes from and where it goes. So is everyone who is born of the Spirit."

Some will not understand you as you move with the Spirit. Don't allow their unpleasant response to deter you from what you know in your heart is true. Don't abort the flow of the Spirit for the desires of men. Peter sums this up nicely:

> Therefore, since Christ suffered for us in the flesh, arm yourselves also with the same mind, for he who has suffered in the flesh has ceased from sin, that he no longer should live the rest of his time in the flesh for the lusts [desires] of men, but for the will of God.
>
> —1 PETER 4:1–2

When you live for the will of God, you will not fulfill the desires of men. As a result, you will suffer in the flesh. Jesus suffered His greatest opposition from the religious leaders. Religious people believe God operates only within the confines of their parameters. They believe they are the only ones who have an "in" with God. If the Master offended religious people as He was led by the Spirit two thousand years ago, those who follow Him will surely offend them.

The apostle Paul's persecution is a good example. Some people in Galatia incorrectly heard that Paul had compromised the gospel of the cross by siding with religious leaders who said circumcision was necessary for salvation. But Paul set them straight.

"Look at me," he said. "I'm being persecuted on every side by religious leaders. Would they be doing this to me if I preached circumcision? The fact that the cross is the only way to salvation offends people, but that is the truth, and there's no way I'm going to preach anything else!" (See Galatians 5:11.)

If anyone challenges the truth of the gospel, it is the time to be offensive without apology. We must determine in our hearts that we will obey the Spirit of God no matter what the cost. Then we will not have to make the choice under pressure because it will have been made.

JESUS OFFENDED
SOME PEOPLE BY OBEYING
HIS FATHER, BUT HE NEVER
CAUSED AN OFFENSE IN
ORDER TO ASSERT HIS
OWN RIGHTS.

I recently read your book *The Bait of Satan,* and I just wanted to tell you that it has totally set me free in an area of my life that I thought I would never be free from. I just wanted to say thank you for writing that book, because it has changed my life!

—C. R., TENNESSEE

CHAPTER 10

LEST WE OFFEND THEM

Therefore let us not judge one another anymore,
but rather resolve this, not to put a stumbling
block or a cause to fall in our brother's way.
—ROMANS 14:13

WE HAVE JUST FINISHED DISCUSSING HOW JESUS OFFENDED many as He traveled and ministered. It appears that almost everywhere He went people were offended. In this chapter I want to look at the flip side of this.

Jesus and His disciples had just returned to Capernaum. They had completed a ministry circuit and had come for a short, but much needed, rest.

If there was any place that could be considered a base for His ministry, it was this city.

While there, Simon Peter was approached by the official in charge of collecting the temple tax. "Does your Teacher not pay the temple tax?" (Matt. 17:24).

Peter answered, "Yes," and went back to discuss it with Jesus.

Jesus anticipated the tax collector's request, so He inquired of Simon Peter, "What do you think, Simon? From whom do the kings of the earth take customs or taxes, from their sons or from strangers?"

"From strangers," Peter told Him.

"Then the sons are free" (Matt. 17:25–26).

Jesus is making a point with Peter that "sons are free." They are not the ones who supply the taxes. They are the ones who enjoy the benefits of the tax. They live in the palace that taxes pay to maintain. The sons eat at the king's table and wear royal apparel, all provided by the tax. They live for free and are freely provided for.

This official received the temple tax. But who was king or owner of the temple? In whose honor was it built? The answer: God the Father. Peter had just received the revelation from God that Jesus was "the Christ, *the Son* of the living God."

On that basis Jesus was asking Peter, "If I am the Son of the One who owns the temple, then am I not free from paying temple tax?" Of course He would be exempt. He would be totally justified in not paying the tax. Yet watch what He says to Simon Peter:

> *Nevertheless, lest we offend them,* go to the sea, cast in a hook, and take the fish that comes up first. And when you have opened its mouth, you will find a piece of money; take that and give it to them for Me and you.
> —MATTHEW 17:27, EMPHASIS ADDED

He had just proven His liberty. But in order not to offend, He said to Peter, "Let's pay it!" It was yet another confirmation of His freedom when He instructed Peter to go and fish and take the first fish that came up; in its mouth he would find money. God the Father even provided the tax money.

Jesus is Lord of the earth. He is the Son of God. The earth and everything in it are created by Him and are subject to Him. Therefore, He knew the money would be in that fish's mouth. He did not have to work for that money because He was the Son. And yet He still chose to pay the tax and not to offend.

Is this the same Jesus we saw in the last chapter offending people and making no apologies for it? He proved He was exempt from the temple tax but said, "Lest we offend them, go and pay it!" It seems as if there is some inconsistency, or is there? Our answer is found in the next verse.

> At that time the disciples came to Jesus, saying, "Who then is greatest in the kingdom of heaven?" Then Jesus called a little child

to Him, set him in the midst of them, and said, "Assuredly, I say to you, unless you are converted and become as little children, you will by no means enter the kingdom of heaven. Therefore whoever humbles himself as this little child is the greatest in the kingdom of heaven."

—Matthew 18:1–4

The key phrase here is "whoever humbles himself." A little later Jesus amplified this by saying:

Whoever desires to become great among you, let him be your servant…just as the Son of Man did not come to be served, but to serve, and to give His life a ransom for many.

—Matthew 20:26–28

Wow! What a statement! He did not come to be served but to serve. He was the Son. He was free. He owed no one anything. He was subject to no man. Yet He chose to use His liberty and freedom to serve.

LIBERATED TO SERVE

We are exhorted in the New Testament as sons of God to imitate our Brother, to have the same attitude we see in Jesus.

For you, brethren, have been called to liberty; only do not use liberty as an opportunity for the flesh, but through love serve one another.

—Galatians 5:13

Another word for liberty is *privilege*. We are not to use our liberty or privileges as children of the living God to serve ourselves. Liberty is to be used to serve others. There is freedom in serving but bondage in slavery. A slave is one who *has* to serve, while a servant is one who *lives* to serve. Let's look at some of the differences between a slave's attitude and a servant's:

- A *slave* has to—a *servant* gets to.
- A *slave* does the minimum requirement—a *servant* reaches the maximum potential.

- A *slave* goes one mile—a *servant* goes the extra mile.
- A *slave* feels robbed—a *servant* gives.
- A *slave* is bound—a *servant* is free.
- A *slave* fights for his rights—a *servant* lays down his rights.

I have seen many Christians serve with a resentful attitude. They give grudgingly and complain as they pay their taxes. They still live as slaves to a law from which they have been set free. They remain slaves in their hearts.

It is most alarming that this law is constructed from the New Testament Scriptures. They do not have the "spirit" in which Jesus gave His commands. They have not realized they were liberated to serve. So they continue to fight for their own benefit rather than for the benefit of others.

Paul gives a vivid example of confronting this attitude in his letters to the Romans and the Corinthians. Liberty for these believers was challenged by food. Paul began by exhorting them to "receive one who is weak in the faith, but not to dispute over doubtful things. For one believes he may eat all things, but he who is weak eats only vegetables" (Rom. 14:1–2).

Jesus had clarified that it was not what goes into the mouth that defiles but what comes out of the mouth. When He made this statement, He made all foods clean to the believer (Mark 7:18–19).

Paul said that there were some believers who were weak in their faith and still could not eat meat for fear of eating food that had been sacrificed to idols. Though Jesus had spoken to the issue, these people still could not eat meat with a clear conscience.

> Therefore concerning the eating of things offered to idols, we know that an idol is nothing in the world....yet for us there is one God, the Father, of whom are all things, and we for Him; and one Lord Jesus Christ, through whom are all things, and through whom we live. However, there is not in everyone that knowledge; for some, with consciousness of the idol, until now eat it as a thing offered to an idol; and their conscience, being weak, is defiled.
>
> —1 CORINTHIANS 8:4, 6–7

In those churches Christians with stronger faith were eating meats of questionable origin in front of weaker saints. This was causing a problem even though Jesus had purified these foods. The weaker ones could not shake the image of the meat on the altar of an idol. The stronger saints knew that an idol was nothing and felt no prick of conscience as they ate.

But it appears that they were more concerned with holding on to their rights as New Testament believers than they were with offending their brethren. Without realizing it they had placed a stumbling block in the path of their weaker brothers. This attitude is not present in the heart of a servant. Look how Paul addressed them:

> Therefore let us not judge one another anymore, but rather resolve this, not to put a stumbling block or a cause to fall in our brother's way....for the kingdom of God is not eating and drinking, but righteousness and peace and joy in the Holy Spirit.
>
> —ROMANS 14:13, 17

He was saying, "Let's remember what the kingdom is really about—righteousness, peace, and joy in the Holy Spirit." All of these benefits were being upset in the new believers. The stronger believers were not using their liberty to serve but as a platform for their "rights." They had knowledge of their New Testament freedom. But knowledge without love destroys.

They did not have the heart of Jesus in this matter. Jesus proved His rights regarding the temple tax to Peter and the rest of the disciples to exemplify the importance of laying down our lives to serve. He never wanted freedom to be a license to demand our rights and cause another to be offended and stumble.

Paul gave this warning to those who had knowledge of their rights in Christ without His heart to serve.

> And because of your knowledge shall the weak brother perish, for whom Christ died? But when you thus sin against the brethren, and wound their weak conscience, you sin against Christ.
>
> —1 CORINTHIANS 8:11–12

We can use our liberty to sin. How? By wounding those of weaker conscience, causing one of Christ's little ones to be offended and stumble.

LAYING DOWN OUR RIGHTS

After Jesus established His liberty in reference to the temple tax, He was careful to charge His disciples with the importance of humility.

> Whoever causes one of these little ones who believe in Me to sin, it would be better for him if a millstone were hung around his neck, and he were drowned in the depth of the sea. Woe to the world because of offenses! For offenses must come, but woe to that man by whom the offense comes!
>
> If your hand or foot causes you to sin, cut it off and cast it from you. It is better for you to enter into life lame or maimed, rather than having two hands or two feet, to be cast into the everlasting fire.
>
> And if your eye causes you to sin, pluck it out and cast it from you. It is better for you to enter into life with one eye, rather than having two eyes, to be cast into hell fire.
>
> Take heed that you do not despise one of these little ones, for I say to you that in heaven their angels always see the face of My Father who is in heaven.
>
> —MATTHEW 18:6–10

This entire chapter of Matthew is about offenses. Jesus is clearly saying to get rid of whatever causes sin, even if it is one of your New Testament privileges. If it causes your weak brother to sin, cut it off before him.

You may wonder, then, why Jesus was offending so many, as we saw in the previous chapter of this book. The answer is simple. Jesus offended some people as a result of obeying the Father and serving others. His offense did not come by demanding His own rights.

The Pharisees were offended when He healed on the Sabbath. His disciples were offended by the truth His Father had Him preach. Mary and Martha were offended when He delayed His return to heal Lazarus. But you will not find Jesus offending others by serving Himself.

Paul in his letter to the Corinthians gave this warning:

> But beware lest somehow this liberty of yours become a stumbling
> block to those who are weak.
>
> —1 CORINTHIANS 8:9

Our liberty has been given to us for serving and laying down our lives. We are to build and not to destroy. Nor was this liberty given for us to heap things on ourselves. Because we have used it in this manner, many today are offended by the lifestyles of Christians.

Again hear the warning given to us in 1 Corinthians 8:9: "But beware lest somehow this liberty of yours become a stumbling block to those who are weak."

Here is an example of how I have seen this commandment broken. On my second ministry trip to Indonesia, I took Lisa, my children, and a babysitter. We arrived in Denpasar, Bali, a resort island.

An elder in the church we were visiting owned a modest hotel in a very noisy section of town. We had traveled a long distance and had had very little sleep. We were exhausted. That night we were awakened several times by loud noises and barking dogs. We only stayed over-night and did not get the rest we needed.

The following day we continued on to Java and ministered for the next two weeks on a very busy schedule. We had only one free day in that two weeks, and that was for travel. In one twenty-four-hour period we ministered five times at a church with thirty thousand members.

At the end of the trip we were scheduled to go back through Bali. The pastor informed us that we would be staying at his elder's hotel again. We were not thrilled about being in those conditions again after two solid weeks of ministry.

At breakfast on the morning we were to leave Java for Bali, a precious lady offered to pay for our accommodations at one of the finest resort hotels in Bali. I was so excited because we would get to rest and stay in a beautiful place.

As we left the restaurant to pack, Lisa told me she did not feel good about accepting this lady's offer. The interpreter and I reasoned with her and said it would be fine. Again on the plane from Java to Bali, she said she didn't think we were doing the right thing.

I was foolish and didn't listen to her. I told her it wouldn't cost the church anything and would be fine. When we arrived in Bali, she pleaded with me at the baggage claim one more time, but I ignored her.

When we met the pastor, I told him we would not need to stay at the elder's hotel because of the woman's offer. He seemed uneasy with what I had said, so I asked him what was wrong.

Fortunately he was open with me and said, "John, this will offend the elder and his family. They've already reserved the room for you, and they're sold out for the evening."

I had also apparently offended the pastor because I did not appreciate what they had arranged for us. Finally I told him we would stay at the elder's hotel and pass up the woman's offer.

The Lord dealt with me about my attitude. I knew the pastor was hurt. I saw that demanding my rights had offended this brother and that it was a sin. I asked for his forgiveness. He forgave me. I hope I don't have to learn that lesson again.

THE EDIFICATION TEST

The apostle Paul, in writing to the Romans, summed up the heart of God in the matter:

> Therefore let us pursue the things which make for peace and the things by which one may edify another.
>
> —ROMANS 14:19

We should make it our aim not to cause another to stumble because of our personal liberty. What we do may even be permissible according to the Scriptures. But ask yourself: Does it seek the edification of another or myself?

> All things are lawful for me, but not all things are helpful; all things are lawful for me, but not all things edify. Let no one seek his own, but each one the other's well-being....Therefore, whether you eat or drink, or whatever you do, do all to the glory of God.
>
> Give no offense, either to the Jews or to the Greeks or to the church of God, just as I also please all men in all things, *not seeking my own profit,* but the profit of many, that they may be saved.
>
> —1 CORINTHIANS 10:23–24, 31–33, EMPHASIS ADDED

I encourage you to allow the Holy Spirit to funnel every area of your life through this Scripture passage. Allow Him to show you any hidden motives or agendas that are for your profit and not for the profit of others. No matter what area of life you might embrace, accept His challenge to live as a servant of all.

Use your liberty in Christ to set others free, not to assert your own rights. That was one of the guidelines of the ministry of Paul, who wrote, "We give no offense in anything, that our ministry may not be blamed" (2 Cor. 6:3).

A PERSON WHO CANNOT
FORGIVE HAS FORGOTTEN HOW
GREAT A DEBT GOD HAS
FORGIVEN THEM.

I've had *The Bait of Satan* in my library for over a year, and I finally began to read it. Immediately I could name the spirit that had taken up residence in my life. I knew beyond a shadow of a doubt that I was being led by the Holy Spirit to read this book. The more I read, the more convicted I became. At church, our pastor implored those who needed to forgive someone to come forward. I went without hesitation to the altar to forgive all those who I felt had offended me, especially my dad. Then I asked my dad to forgive me. I am thankful that he did, and now I am free! Thank you for that book!

—R. P., VIRGINIA

CHAPTER 11

FORGIVENESS: YOU DON'T GIVE—YOU DON'T GET

*Therefore I say to you, whatever things you ask when you
pray, believe that you receive them, and you will have them.
And whenever you stand praying, if you have anything
against anyone, forgive him, that your Father in heaven may
also forgive you your trespasses. But if you do not forgive,
neither will your Father in heaven forgive your trespasses.*
—MARK 11:24–26

FOR THE REMAINDER OF THE BOOK I WANT TO TURN OUR ATTEN-
tion to the consequences of refusing to let go of offense and how
to get free from it.

Jesus meant what He said, "But if you do not forgive, neither will
your Father in heaven forgive your trespasses." We live in a culture
where we don't always mean what we say. Consequently we do not
believe others mean what they say to us. A person's word is not taken
seriously.

It begins in childhood. A parent tells a child, "If you do that again,
you'll get a spanking." The child not only does it again but several
times more after that. Following each episode the child receives the

same warning from his parent. Usually no corrective action is taken. If correction does take place, it is either lighter than what was promised or more severe because the parent is frustrated.

Both responses send a message to the child that you don't mean what you say or what you say isn't true. The child learns to think that not everything authority figures say is true. So he becomes confused about when and if he should take authority figures seriously. This attitude is projected onto other areas of his life. He views his teachers, friends, leaders, and bosses through this same frame of reference. By the time he becomes an adult he has accepted this as normal. His conversations now consist of promises and statements in which he says things he doesn't mean.

Let me give you a hypothetical example of a typical conversation. Jim sees Tom, whom he knows but hasn't talked to in a while. He is in a hurry and thinks, "Oh, no. I can't believe I am running into Tom. I don't have time to talk."

The two men look at each other.

Jim says, "Praise the Lord, brother. It is good to see you."

They talk a short while. Since Jim is in a hurry, he finishes by saying, "We need to get together sometime for lunch."

First, Jim was not excited about seeing Tom because he was in a hurry. Second, he was not thinking about the Lord and greeted Tom with "Praise the Lord." Third, he had no intention of following up on that lunch invitation. It was just a means of getting away quicker and easing his conscience in the process. So Jim really meant nothing he said in that conversation.

Real situations like this occur every day. Today most people don't mean a fourth of what they say. So is it any wonder we have a difficult time knowing when to take a person at his or her word?

But when Jesus speaks, He wants us to take Him seriously. We cannot view what He says the way we view the other authorities or relations in our lives. When He says something, He means it. He is faithful even when we are faithless. He walks at a level of truth and integrity that transcends our culture or society. So when Jesus said, "But if you do not forgive, neither will your Father in heaven forgive your trespasses," He meant it.

To take this one step further, He does not say this just once in the Gospels but many times. He was emphasizing the importance of this warning. Let's look at a few of these statements He made on different occasions.

> For if you forgive men their trespasses, your heavenly Father will also forgive you. But if you do not forgive men their trespasses, neither will your Father forgive your trespasses.
>
> —MATTHEW 6:14–15

And again:

> Forgive, and you will be forgiven.
>
> —LUKE 6:37

Again in the Lord's Prayer we read:

> And forgive us our debts, *as we forgive* our debtors.
>
> —MATTHEW 6:12, EMPHASIS ADDED

I wonder how many Christians would want God to forgive them in the same way they have forgiven those who have offended them. Yet this is exactly the way in which they will be forgiven. Because unforgiveness is so rampant in our churches, we do not want to take these words of Jesus so seriously. Rampant or not, truth does not change. The way we forgive, release, and restore another person is the way we will be forgiven.

FORGIVENESS AND SPIRITUAL GROWTH

Lisa and I have also seen many examples of the trap of unforgiveness in our own ministry. When I was ministering for the first time in Indonesia, I stayed in the home of a wealthy businessman. Even though he and his family attended the church where I was ministering, they were not saved.

During the week I was there, his wife was saved; he was next, and then all three children. There was deliverance, and the entire atmosphere in the house was changed. Great joy filled their home.

When they learned I would be returning to Indonesia with my wife, they invited us to stay with them and offered to pay for the airline tickets of my three children and a babysitter.

We arrived and ministered ten times in their church. I preached on repentance and the presence of God. We sensed His presence in the services, with tears flowing and cries of deliverance throughout.

The entire family was again ministered to. The husband's mother, who lived in the same city, attended every service. She had also contributed a large amount of money to the children's airline tickets.

Near the end of the week, this man's mother looked me straight in the eye and asked, "John, why have I never felt the presence of God?"

We had just finished breakfast, and everyone else had already left the table.

"I have been to every service," she continued, "and have listened closely to everything you've said. I have come to the front repenting, yet I have not felt the presence of God once. Not only that, but I have never felt the presence of God at any other time either."

I talked with her for a while and then said, "Let's pray for you to be filled with God's Spirit." I laid my hands upon her and prayed for her to receive the Holy Spirit, but there was no sense of God's presence at all.

Then God spoke to my spirit. "She is holding unforgiveness against her husband. Tell her to forgive him."

I took my hands off her. I knew her husband was dead, but I looked at her and said, "The Lord shows me you are holding unforgiveness against your husband."

"Yes, I am," she agreed. "But I have done my best to forgive him."

Then she told me about the horrible things he had done to her. I could see why she wrestled with forgiving him.

But I said to her, "For you to receive from God you must forgive," and explained what Jesus taught about forgiveness.

"You cannot forgive him in your own strength. You must take this before God and first ask God to forgive you. Then you can forgive your husband. Are you willing to release your husband?" I asked.

"Yes," she answered.

I led her in a simple prayer: "Father in heaven, in Jesus's name I ask Your forgiveness for holding unforgiveness against my husband. Lord, I know I cannot forgive him in my own strength. I have already failed, but before You now I release my husband from my heart. I forgive him."

No sooner had she said those words than tears began to flow down her cheeks.

"Lift up your hands and speak in tongues," I urged her.

For the first time she prayed in a beautiful heavenly language. We had such a strong sense of the presence of the Lord at the breakfast table that we were overwhelmed and awed by it. She wept for about five minutes. We talked a little while, then I encouraged her to enjoy the presence of the Lord. She continued to worship Him, and I left her alone.

When news reached her son and daughter-in-law, they were shocked. The son said he had never seen his mother cry.

She herself did not remember the last time she had cried. "Even when my husband died I did not cry."

In the service that night she was baptized in water. For the next three days a glow and a sweet smile radiated from her face. I did not remember seeing her smile before that. She would not forgive and was therefore imprisoned by unforgiveness. But once she released her husband and forgave him, she received the power of the Lord in her life and became aware of His presence.

THE UNFORGIVING SERVANT

In Matthew 18 Jesus sheds further light on the bondage of unforgiveness and offense. He was teaching the disciples how to be reconciled with a brother who had offended them. (We will discuss reconciliation in a later chapter.)

Peter asked, "Lord, how often shall my brother sin against me, and I forgive him? Up to seven times?" (Matt. 18:21). He thought he was being generous.

Peter liked to take things to the extreme. He was the one who had said, "Let's build three tabernacles, one for You, Jesus, one for Moses, and one for Elijah," on the Mount of Transfiguration. (See Matthew 17:4.) Now he thought he was being magnanimous. *I'll impress the Master with my willingness to forgive seven times.*

But he received a shocking reply. Jesus blew away what Peter considered generous: "I do not say to you, up to seven times, but up to *seventy times seven*" (Matt. 18:21–22, emphasis added). In other words, forgive as God does, without limits.

Then Jesus told a parable to emphasize His point.

> Therefore the kingdom of heaven is like a certain king who wanted to settle accounts with his servants. And when he had begun to settle accounts, one was brought to him who owed him ten thousand talents.
>
> —MATTHEW 18:23–24

To understand the enormity of what Jesus was saying, we must know what a talent was. A talent was a unit of measure. It was used to measure gold (2 Sam. 12:30), silver (1 Kings 20:39), and other metals and commodities. In this parable it represents a debt, so we can be safe in assuming He was referring to a unit of exchange such as gold or silver. Let's say gold.

The common talent was equivalent to approximately seventy-five pounds. It was the full weight that a man could carry. (See 2 Kings 5:23.) Ten thousand talents would be approximately 750,000 pounds or 375 tons. So this servant owed the king 375 tons of gold.

At the present time, the price of gold is roughly $1,210 an ounce. In today's market a talent of gold would be worth $1.4 million. Therefore, ten thousand talents of gold is worth $14.5 billion. This servant owed his king $14.5 billion!

Jesus was emphasizing here that this servant owed a debt he could never pay. We read:

> But as he was not able to pay, his master commanded that he be sold, with his wife and children and all that he had, and that payment be made. The servant therefore fell down before him, saying, "Master, have patience with me, and I will pay you all." Then the master of that servant was moved with compassion, released him, and forgave him the debt.
>
> —MATTHEW 18:25–27

Now let's look at how this parable applies to being offended. When an offense occurs, a debt is owed. You have heard it said, "He'll pay for this." So forgiveness is like the cancellation of a debt.

The king represents God the Father, who forgave this servant a debt that was impossible for him to pay. In Colossians 2:13–14 we find, "And you, being dead in your trespasses and the uncircumcision of your flesh, He has made alive together with Him, having forgiven you all trespasses, having wiped out the handwriting of [*certificate of debt* with its] requirements that was against us, which was contrary to us. And He has taken it out of the way, having nailed it to the cross."[1]

The debt we were forgiven was unpayable. There was no way we could ever repay God what we owed Him. Our offense was overwhelming. So God gave salvation as a gift. Jesus paid the certificate of debt that was against us. We can see the parallel between this servant's relationship to his king and our relationship with God.

> But that servant went out and found one of his fellow servants who owed him a hundred denarii; and he laid hands on him and took him by the throat, saying, "Pay me what you owe!"
> —MATTHEW 18:28

A denarius was approximately equal to a laborer's daily wage.[2] So at today's wages, one hundred denarii would be worth about four thousand dollars. Now continue to read:

> So his fellow servant fell down at his feet and begged him, saying, "Have patience with me, and I will pay you all." And he would not, but went and threw him into prison till he should pay the debt.
> —MATTHEW 18:29–30

One of his fellow servants owed him a sizable sum of money—one-third of a year's wages. How would you like it if you were missing a third of your salary? But remember that this man was forgiven a debt of $14.5 billion. That's more money than he could earn in a lifetime!

The offenses we hold against each other compared to our offenses against God are like $4,000 compared to $14.5 billion. We may have been treated badly by someone else, but it does not compare with our transgressions against God.

You may feel no one has it as bad as you do. But you don't realize how badly Jesus was treated. He was innocent, a blameless lamb that was slain.

A person who cannot forgive has forgotten the great debt for which they were forgiven. When you realize that Jesus delivered you from eternal death and torment, you will release others unconditionally. (We'll talk about how to walk through this in chapter 13.)

There is nothing worse than eternity in a lake of fire. There is no relief, the worm does not die, and the fire is not quenched. That was our destination until God forgave us through the death of His Son, Jesus Christ. Hallelujah! If you have a hard time forgiving, think of the reality of hell and the love of God that saved you from it.

LESSONS FOR BELIEVERS

Let's continue the parable:

> So when his fellow servants saw what had been done, they were very grieved, and came and told their master all that had been done. Then his master, after he had called him, said to him, "You wicked servant! I forgave you all that debt because you begged me. Should you not also have had compassion on your fellow servant, just as I had pity on you?"
>
> —Matthew 18:31–33

Jesus was not referring to unbelievers in this parable. He was talking about servants of the king. This man already had a great debt forgiven (salvation) and was called the master's "servant." The one he would not forgive was a "fellow servant." So we can conclude that this is the fate of a believer who refuses to forgive.

> And his master was angry, and delivered him to the torturers until he should pay all that was due to him. So My heavenly Father also will do to you if each of you, from his heart, does not forgive his brother his trespasses.
>
> —Matthew 18:34–35

These verses have three major points.

1. The unforgiving servant is turned over to torture.
2. He has to pay off the original debt: 375 tons of gold.
3. God the Father will do the same to any believer who does not forgive a brother's offense.

1. The unforgiving servant is turned over to torture.

Webster's dictionary defines *torture* as "agony of body or mind" or "the infliction of intense pain to punish, coerce, or afford sadistic pleasure."[3]

The instigators of this torture are demon spirits. God gives the "torturers" permission to inflict pain and agony of body and mind at will even if we are believers. I have often prayed for people in services who could not receive healing, comfort, or deliverance, all because they would not release others and forgive from their hearts.

Medical doctors and scientists have linked unforgiveness and bitterness with certain diseases, such as arthritis and cancer. Many cases of mental sickness are tied to bitter unforgiveness.

Forgiveness is usually denied to other people, but sometimes it is denied to oneself. Jesus said, "If you have anything against anyone, forgive…" (See Matthew 5:24.) Anyone includes you! If God forgave you, who are you not to forgive one He has forgiven, even if it is you?

2. The unforgiving servant had to pay the original unpayable debt.

He was required to do the impossible. It is like our being required to pay the debt Jesus paid at Calvary.

"Wait a minute," you say. "I thought that once a person prayed the sinner's prayer and committed his life to Jesus he could never be lost."

If you believe that, then explain why Peter wrote the following:

> For if, after they have escaped the pollutions of the world through the knowledge of the Lord and Savior Jesus Christ, they are again entangled in them and overcome, the latter end is worse for them than the beginning. *For it would have been better for them not to have known the way of righteousness,* than having known it, to turn from the holy commandment delivered to them.
>
> —2 PETER 2:20–21, EMPHASIS ADDED

Peter was talking about people who had escaped sin (pollutions of the world) through salvation in Jesus Christ. However, they were again entangled by sin (which could be unforgiveness) and overcome by it. To be overcome meant they did not return to the Lord and repent of their willful sin. Peter stated that turning from righteousness was worse than never knowing it at all. In other words, God is saying it is better never to have gotten saved than to receive the gift of eternal life and then turn from it permanently.

Jude also described people in the church who were "twice dead" (Jude 12–13). To be twice dead means you were once dead without Christ, then you were made alive by receiving Him, then you died again by departing from His ways permanently.

We see that many will come to Jesus justifying themselves by saying: "'Lord, Lord, have we not prophesied in Your name, cast out demons in Your name, and done many wonders in Your name?' And then I will declare to them, 'I never knew you; depart from Me, you who practice lawlessness!'" (Matt. 7:22–23). They knew Him. They called Him Lord and did miracles in His name. But He did not know them.

Whom will Jesus know? The apostle Paul wrote, "But if anyone loves God, this one is known by Him" (1 Cor. 8:3). God knows those who love Him.

You may say, "I love God. I just don't love this brother who has hurt me." Then you are deceived, and you do not love God, for it is written, "If someone says, 'I love God,' and hates his brother…whom he has seen, how can he love God whom he has not seen?" (1 John 4:20). Deception is a terrible thing, for the deceived believes with all of his heart that he is right. He believes he is one way when he is really another. A person who refuses to obey the Word deceives his own heart.

Isn't it interesting that "many" will expect to enter heaven and be refused and that Jesus said many would be offended in the last days (Matt. 24:10)? Could these two groups include the same people?

Some believers are so tormented by unforgiveness that they may hope death will bring relief. But this is not true. We must deal with unforgiveness now or be called upon to pay the unpayable.

3. God the Father will do this to any believer who refuses to forgive from the heart—no matter how great the hurt or offense.

Jesus was very specific, making sure we understood this parable. In almost every parable Jesus did not offer the interpretation unless His disciples asked for it. In this case, however, He wanted no question about the severity of judgment for those who refused to forgive.

In many other instances Jesus also made it clear that if we would not forgive we would not be forgiven. Remember that He is not like us; He means what He says.

This is not often found in the church. Instead, excuses are given for harboring unforgiveness. Unforgiveness is considered to be a lesser sin than homosexuality, adultery, theft, drunkenness, and so on. But those who practice it will not inherit the kingdom of God along with those who practice the other sins.

Some may think this is a hard message, but I see it as a message of mercy and warning, not of harsh judgment. Would you rather be convicted by the Holy Spirit now and experience genuine repentance and forgiveness? Or would you rather refuse to forgive and hear the Master say, "Depart," when you can no longer repent?

WE ARE TO BE
SO FAR REMOVED FROM
AVENGING OURSELVES THAT
WE WILLINGLY RISK BEING TAKEN
ADVANTAGE OF AGAIN.

I thank God for your obedience in writing *The Bait of Satan*. This book is so anointed that the Spirit of the Lord dealt with me the entire time while I read it, which only took a couple of days. This book has changed my life completely. I have been freed from the chains of offenses and will continue to exercise my heart, mind, and emotions to remain free.

—L. M., SOUTH CAROLINA

CHAPTER 12

REVENGE: THE TRAP

*Repay no one evil for evil. Have regard for
good things in the sight of all men.*
—ROMANS 12:17

A S WE CLEARLY SAW IN THE LAST CHAPTER, HOLDING ON TO
an offense of unforgiveness is like holding a debt against
someone. When one person is wronged by another, he believes that
a debt is owed to him. He expects a payment of some sort, whether
monetary or not.

Our court system exists to avenge wronged or injured parties.
Lawsuits result from people trying to satisfy their debts. When a
person has been hurt by another, human justice says, "They will stand
trial for what they have done and pay if found guilty." The unforgiving servant wanted his fellow servant to pay what he owed, so he
sought his compensation in the court of law. This is not the way of
righteousness.

> Beloved, do not avenge yourselves, but rather give place to wrath; for
> it is written, "Vengeance is Mine, I will repay," says the Lord.
> —ROMANS 12:19

It is unrighteous for us as children of God to avenge ourselves.
But that is exactly what we are seeking when we refuse to forgive. We

desire, seek, plan, and carry out revenge. We will not forgive until the debt is paid in full, and only we can determine the acceptable compensation. When we seek to correct the wrong done to us, we set ourselves up as judges. But we know:

> There is one Lawgiver, who is able to save and to destroy. Who are you to judge another? Do not grumble against one another, brethren, lest you be condemned. Behold, the Judge is standing at the door!
> —James 4:12; 5:9

God is the just Judge. He will pass righteous judgment. But He will repay according to righteousness. If someone has done wrong and genuinely repents, Jesus's work at Calvary erases the debt.

You may say, "But the wrong was done to me, not to Jesus!"

Yes, but you don't realize the wrong you did to Him. An innocent victim, He bore no guilt while every other human had sinned and was condemned to die. Each one of us has broken laws of God that transcend the laws of the land. All of us should be condemned to death by the hand of the highest court in the universe if justice is served.

You may have done nothing to provoke the wrong you incurred at the hand of another. But if you contrast what was done to you with what you've been forgiven of, there is no comparison. It would not even put a dent in the debt you owe! If you feel cheated, you have lost your concept of the mercy extended you.

NO GRAY GRUDGE AREAS

Under the Old Testament covenant, if you trespassed against me, I had legal rights to bring the same back on you. Permission was granted to collect on debts, repaying evil for evil. (See Leviticus 24:19; Exodus 21:23–25.) Law was supreme. Jesus had not yet died to set them free.

Look how He addresses new covenant believers.

> *You have heard that it was said*, "An eye for an eye and a tooth for a tooth." *But I tell you not* to resist an evil person. But whoever slaps you on your right cheek, turn the other to him also. If anyone wants to sue you and take away your tunic, let him have your cloak also. And whoever compels you to go one mile, go with him two. Give

to him who asks you, and from him who wants to borrow from you
do not turn away.

—MATTHEW 5:38–42, EMPHASIS ADDED

Jesus eliminates any gray areas for grudges. In fact He says that
our attitude is to be so far removed from avenging ourselves that we
are willing to open ourselves to the possibility of being taken advantage of again.

When we seek to correct the wrong done to us, we set ourselves
up as a judge. The unforgiving servant in Matthew 18 did this when
he put his fellow servant in jail. In turn this unforgiving servant was
turned over to the tormentors, and his family sold, until he should
pay all.

We must make room and give place to the just Judge. He rewards
righteously. Only He avenges in righteousness.

I was ministering on the subject of offenses at a church in Tampa,
Florida. Afterward a woman came to me. She said she had forgiven
her ex-husband for all he'd done. But as she listened to me talk about
releasing offenses, she realized she still did not have peace inside and
was very uncomfortable.

"You still have not forgiven him," I told her gently.

"Yes, I have," she said. "I have cried tears of forgiveness."

"You may have cried, but you still have not released him."

She insisted that I was wrong and that she had forgiven him. "I
don't want anything from him. I have released him."

"Tell me what he did to you," I asked.

"My husband and I pastored a church. He left me and our three
boys and ran away with a prominent woman in the church." Tears
formed in her eyes. "He said he'd missed God by marrying me because
it was God's perfect will for him to marry the woman he ran away
with. He told me she was an asset to his ministry because she was
much more supportive. He said I was a hindrance. He said I was critical. He put all the blame of the marriage breakup on me. He has
never come back and admitted that any of it was his fault."

This man was obviously deceived and had greatly wronged his wife
and family. She had suffered much from his actions and was waiting
for him to pay back a debt. The debt was not alimony or child support,
for her new husband was providing all this for her. The debt she wanted

him to pay was to admit that he had been wrong and she had been right.

"You won't forgive him until he comes to you and says that he was wrong, that it was his fault, not yours, and then asks for your forgiveness. This is the unfulfilled payment that has kept you bound," I pointed out to her.

If Jesus had waited for us to come to Him and apologize, saying, "We were wrong. You were right. Forgive us," He would *not* have forgiven us from the cross. As He hung on the cross, He cried out, "Father, forgive them, for they do not know what they do" (Luke 23:34). He forgave us before we came to Him confessing our offense against Him. We are admonished by the words of the apostle Paul: "Even as Christ forgave you, so you also must do" (Col. 3:13). And "be kind to one another, tenderhearted, forgiving one another, even as God in Christ forgave you" (Eph. 4:32).

When I told this woman, "You won't forgive him until he says, 'I was wrong—you were right,'" tears streamed down her face. What she wanted seemed small in comparison to all the pain he had brought to her and her children. But she was in bondage to human justice. She had set herself up as a judge, claiming her right to the debt and waiting for payment. This offense had hindered her relationship with her new husband. It had also affected her relationship with all male authorities because her former husband had been her pastor as well.

Often Jesus likened the condition of our hearts to that of soil. We are admonished to be rooted and grounded in the love of God. The seed of God's Word will then take root in our hearts and grow and eventually produce the fruit of righteousness. This fruit is love, joy, peace, long-suffering, kindness, goodness, faithfulness, gentleness, and self-control. (See Galatians 5:22–23.)

But ground will produce only what is planted in it. If we plant seeds of debt, unforgiveness, and offense, another root will spring up in place of the love of God. It is called the root of bitterness.

Francis Frangipane gave an excellent definition of bitterness: "Bitterness is unfulfilled revenge."[1] It is produced when revenge is not satisfied to the degree we desire.

The writer of the Book of Hebrews spoke directly about this issue.

Pursue peace with all people, and holiness, without which no one will see the Lord: looking carefully lest anyone fall short of the grace of God; lest any *root of bitterness* springing up cause trouble, and by this *many become defiled.*

—HEBREWS 12:14–15, EMPHASIS ADDED

Notice the words "many become defiled." Could this again be the "many" Jesus said would be offended in the last days? (See Matthew 24:10.)

Bitterness is a root. If roots are nursed—watered, protected, fed, and given attention—they increase in depth and strength. If not dealt with quickly, roots are hard to pull up. The strength of the offense will continue to grow. We are therefore exhorted not to let the sun go down on our wrath. (See Ephesians 4:26.) Now instead of the fruit of righteousness being produced, we will see a harvest of anger, resentment, jealousy, hatred, strife, and discord. Jesus called these evil fruits. (See Matthew 7:19–20.)

The Bible says a person who does not pursue peace by releasing offenses will eventually become defiled. That which is precious will end up being corrupted by the vileness of unforgiveness.

A POTENTIAL KING DEFILED

Earlier in the book we looked at how David remained loyal to King Saul even when Saul was not loyal to David. David did not seek to avenge himself, even when given the opportunity twice. David was a man after the heart of God. He let God judge between Saul and him. When God's judgment fell upon Saul, David did not rejoice. He grieved over Saul for he held no bitterness toward him.

After Saul's death, David ascended to the throne. He strengthened the nation, enjoyed military and financial success, and held the throne securely. He married many wives who bore him children, including Amnon, his oldest son, and Absalom, his third-born son.

David's son Amnon committed a wicked offense against his half sister Tamar, who was Absalom's sister. He pretended to be ill and asked his father to send Tamar to serve him food. When she did, he ordered the servants out and raped her. He then despised her and had her removed from his sight. He had disgraced a virgin royal princess, devastating her life with shame. (See 2 Samuel 13.)

Without saying a word to his half brother, Absalom brought his sister into his own home and provided for her. But he hated Amnon for defiling Tamar.

Absalom expected his father to punish his half brother. King David was outraged when he heard of Amnon's wickedness, but he took no course of action. Absalom was devastated by his father's lack of justice.

Tamar had once worn the royal robes that were reserved for the king's virgin daughters; now she was robed in shame. She was a beautiful girl and had probably been held in high esteem by the people. Now she lived in seclusion, unable to marry because she was no longer a virgin.

It was unfair. She had attended Amnon at the king's command, and she was raped. Her life was over, while the man who committed this atrocity lived as if nothing had happened. She bore the weight of it all, her life in shambles.

Day after day Absalom saw his grieving sister. The perfect existence of a princess had become a nightmare. Absalom waited a year for his father to do something, but David did nothing. Absalom was offended by his father, and he hated the wicked Amnon.

After two years his hatred for Amnon birthed a plot to murder him. "I will avenge my sister since the proper authority chooses to do nothing," Absalom probably thought.

He threw a feast for all the king's sons. When Amnon did not suspect him, Absalom had him killed. Absalom then fled to Geshur, his revenge accomplished against Amnon. But the offense he carried against his father burned stronger, especially while he was away from the palace.

Absalom's thoughts were poisoned with bitterness. He became an expert critic of David's weaknesses. Yet he hoped his father would call for him. David did not. This fueled Absalom's resentment.

Perhaps these were his thoughts: "My father is hailed by the people, but they are blind to his true nature. He is only a self-seeking man who uses God as a cover-up. Why, he is worse than King Saul! Saul lost his throne for not killing the king of the Amalekites and sparing a few of their best sheep and oxen. My father has committed adultery with the wife of one of his most loyal men. Then he covered his sin by killing the man who was loyal to him. He is a murderer and an adulterer—that is why he did not punish Amnon! And he covers all this up with his fake worship of Jehovah."

Absalom stayed in Geshur for three years. David had been comforted over the death of his son Amnon, and Joab had convinced the king to bring Absalom home. But David still refused to meet Absalom face-to-face. Two more years went by, and David finally returned Absalom to favor and granted him full privileges again. But the offense in Absalom's heart stayed just as strong.

Absalom was an expert in appearances. Before he murdered Amnon, "Absalom spoke to his brother Amnon neither good nor bad. For Absalom hated Amnon" (2 Sam. 13:22). Many people are able to hide their offense and hatred as Absalom did.

Out of this offended critical attitude, he began to draw to himself anyone who was discontented. He made himself available to all Israel, taking time to listen to their complaints. He would lament that things would be different if only he were king. He judged their cases since it appeared the king had no time for them. Perhaps Absalom judged their cases because he felt he had not been served justice in his own.

He seemed to be concerned for the people. The Bible says Absalom stole the hearts of Israel from his father, David. But was he genuinely concerned for them, or was he seeking a way to overthrow David, the one who had offended him?

EXPERTS ON ERROR

Absalom drew Israel to him and rose up against David. King David had to flee Jerusalem for his life. It looked as if Absalom would establish his own kingdom. Instead, he was killed as he pursued David, even though David had ordered that he remain untouched.

Absalom was, in fact, killed by his own bitterness and offense. The man with so much potential, heir to the throne, died in his prime because he refused to release the debt he thought his father owed. He ended up defiled.

Assistants to leaders in a church often become offended by the person they serve. They soon become critical—experts at all that is wrong with their leader or those he or she appoints. They become offended. Their sight is distorted. They see from a totally different perspective than God's.

They believe their mission in life is to deliver those around them from an unfair leader. They win the hearts of the disgruntled, discontent, and ignorant, and before they know it they end up splitting or dividing the church or ministry. Just like Absalom.

Sometimes their observations are correct. Perhaps David *should have* taken action against Amnon. Perhaps a leader has areas of error. Who is the judge—you or the Lord? Remember that if you sow strife, you will reap it.

What happened to Absalom and what happens in modern ministries is a process that takes time. We are often unaware that an offense has entered our hearts. The root of bitterness is barely noticeable as it develops. But as it is nursed it will grow and be strengthened. As the writer of Hebrews exhorts, we are to look "carefully…lest any root of bitterness springing up cause trouble, and by this many become defiled" (Heb. 12:15).

We must examine our hearts and open ourselves to the correction of the Lord, for only His Word can discern the thoughts and intentions of our hearts. The Holy Spirit convicts as He speaks through one's conscience. We must not ignore His conviction or quench Him. If anyone has done this, repent before God, and open your heart to His correction.

A minister once asked me if he had acted as an Absalom or a David in something he had done. He had served as an assistant to a pastor in a city, and the pastor fired him. It seemed that the senior pastor was jealous and afraid of this young man because God's hand was on him.

A year later the minister who was fired believed the Lord wanted him to start a church on the other side of the city. So he did, and some of the people from the church he had left came over to join him. He was troubled because he did not want to act as an Absalom, but he was apparently not offended with his former leader. He started the new church from the leading of the Lord, not out of responding to the lack of care at the other church.

I pointed out to him the difference between Absalom and David. Absalom stole the hearts of others because he was offended with his leader. David encouraged others to stay loyal to Saul even though Saul was attacking him. Absalom took men with him; David left alone.

"Did you leave your church alone?" I asked him. "Did you do anything to encourage people to come with you or support you?"

"I left alone and did nothing to draw people with me," he said.

"That's fine. You have acted as a David. Make sure the people who come to you are not offended with your former pastor, and if they are, lead them to freedom and healing."

This man's church is now prospering. What I appreciated so much about him was that he was not afraid to examine his own heart. Not only that, but also he submitted himself to godly counsel. It was more important to him that he was submitted to God's way than that he was proven "right."

Do not be afraid to allow the Holy Spirit to reveal any unforgiveness or bitterness. The longer you hide it, the stronger it will become and the harder your heart will grow. Stay tenderhearted. How?

> Let all bitterness, wrath, anger, clamor, and evil speaking be put away from you, with all malice. And be kind to one another, tenderhearted, forgiving one another, even as God in Christ forgave you.
>
> —EPHESIANS 4:31–32

YOU GROW MORE
FROM THE MOST CHALLENGING
OFFENSES—THE ONES FOR
WHICH YOU HAVE NOT
BEEN TRAINED.

I got *The Bait of Satan!* What a blessing that book is. I have recommended it to many. God really used it in my life. Thanks!

—S. T., GEORGIA

CHAPTER 13

ESCAPING THE TRAP

And herein do I exercise myself, to have always a
conscience void of offence toward God, and toward men.
—ACTS 24:16, KJV

I T TAKES EFFORT TO STAY FREE FROM OFFENSE. PAUL COMPARES IT
to exercising. If we exercise our bodies we are less prone to injury.
While in Hawaii I climbed a wall to take a picture. When I did, I
pulled a group of muscles in my knee and could not walk for four days.

"If you had been exercising regularly," the physical therapist told
me, "this would not have happened. Because your muscles are out of
shape, you are prone to injury."

Once I was able to walk, another expert instructed me, "You must
do these exercises to bring your knee muscles back into proper shape
and condition." It took a few months to get my knee back to normal.

The Greek word in Acts 24:16 for *exercise* is *askeo*. *Vine's Exposi-*
tory Dictionary defines *exercise* as "to take pains, endeavor, exercise by
training or discipline."[1]

Sometimes others offend us, and it is not hard to forgive. We have
exercised our hearts so they are in condition to handle the offense;
therefore, no injury or permanent damage results.

Many people could have climbed that wall in Hawaii and not been
injured because they were in shape. Likewise, some are conditioned

to obey God by exercising their hearts. Our degree of maturity determines how well we will handle an offense without injury.

Some offenses will be more challenging than those for which we've been trained. This extra strain may cause a wound or injury after which we will have to exercise spiritually to be free and healed again. But the result will be worth the effort.

In this chapter I will address these extreme, intense offenses that require more effort to resolve.

An incident occurred in my life involving someone in the ministry. This extreme offense I experienced was not isolated but was one of several with this person that intensified over a year and a half.

Everyone around me knew what was going on. "Aren't you hurt?" they asked me. "What are you going to do? Are you just going to stand back and take it?"

"I'm fine," I said. "It hasn't affected me. I'm going on with the call on my life."

But my answer was nothing more than pride. I was extremely hurt but denied it, even to myself. I would spend hours trying to figure out how all this could happen to me. I was in shock, numb, and amazed. But I suppressed these thoughts and put on a strong front when in reality I was weak and deeply injured.

Months went by. Everything seemed dry, the ministry was stale, my prayer closet was lonely, and I was in torment. I fought devils daily. I thought all the resistance was because of the call on my life, but in actuality it was the torment from my unforgiveness. Every time I was around this man I came away feeling spiritually beat up.

Then came the morning I will never forget. I was sitting on the deck in my backyard praying. "Lord, am I hurt?" I asked.

No sooner had these words left my lips when I heard a shout deep in my spirit: *Yes!*

God wanted to make sure I knew I was hurt.

"God, please help me get out of this hurt and offense," I pleaded. "It is too much for me to handle."

This was exactly where the Lord wanted me—at the end of myself. Too often we try to do things in the strength of our souls. This does not cause us to grow spiritually. Instead, we become more susceptible to falling.

The first step to healing and freedom is to recognize you are hurt. Often pride does not want us to admit we are hurt and offended. Once I admitted my true condition, I sought the Lord and was open to His correction.

I sensed that the Lord wanted me to fast for a few days. Fasting would put me in a position of being sensitive to the voice of His Spirit and provide other benefits as well.

> Is this not the fast that I have chosen: To loose the bonds of wickedness, to undo the heavy burdens, to let the oppressed go free, and that you break every yoke?
>
> —ISAIAH 58:6

I was ready for those bonds of wickedness to be broken and to be free from oppression.

A few days later I was attending a funeral service. The man who had offended me was there also. I watched him from the back of the church and began to weep.

"Lord, I forgive him. I release him from everything he has done." Immediately I felt the burden lift. I had forgiven him. What relief flooded me!

But this was only the beginning of my road to recovery. In my heart I had forgiven, but I wasn't aware of the extent of the wound. I was still vulnerable and could be hurt again. It was just like recovering from a physical injury. I needed to exercise, to strengthen my heart, mind, and emotions to prevent any future injuries.

WHAT ABOUT RELAPSES?

A few months went by. Occasionally I had to fight off some of the same thoughts I'd had before I forgave. A person hurt in the same manner might bring their complaint to me, or perhaps I would see the man or hear his name. I rejected these thoughts as soon as I noticed them and cast them down. (See 2 Corinthians 10:5.) This was my exercising or striving to stay free.

Finally I asked the Lord how to keep these thoughts from drawing me back into unforgiveness. I knew He desired a higher level of freedom for me, and I did not want to live the rest of my life holding offense at arm's length. The Lord instructed me to pray for the man who had hurt me, reminding me of His words:

> But I say to you, love your enemies, bless those who curse you, do good to those who hate you, and pray for those who spitefully use you and persecute you.
>
> —MATTHEW 5:44

So I prayed. At first it was in a dry, monotone voice, without a hint of passion. Out of obligation I would add, "Lord, bless him. Give him a good day. Help him in all he does. In Jesus's name, amen."

This continued for a few weeks. I seemed to be getting nowhere. Then one morning the Lord impressed Psalm 35 upon me. I had no idea what was in Psalm 35, so I turned to it and began to read. When I got halfway, I saw my situation.

> Fierce witnesses rise up; they ask me things that I do not know. They reward me evil for good, to the sorrow of my soul.
>
> —PSALM 35:11–12

I could identify with David. In my opinion both the man and some of his associates had rewarded me evil for good. My soul was definitely in sorrow. God was using this psalm to point out my battle for those last few years. One passage made me jump almost high enough to hit the ceiling.

> *But as for me,* when they were sick, my clothing was sackcloth; I humbled myself with fasting; and my prayer would return to my own heart. I paced about as though he were my friend or brother; I bowed down heavily, as one who mourns for his mother.
>
> —PSALM 35:13–14, EMPHASIS ADDED

David said that these men were trying to destroy him. They attacked him with evil when he had done nothing to merit it.

Then came my answer: *"But as for me . . ."*

David's response was not based on the actions of others. Determined to do what was right, he prayed for them as if they were his close brothers or as one grieving the loss of a mother. God was showing me how to pray for this man: "Pray the very things for him that you want Me to do for you!"

Now my prayers totally changed. It was no longer, "God bless him and give him a good day." It became infused with life. I prayed, "Lord, reveal Yourself to him in a greater way. Bless him with Your presence. Let him know You more intimately. May he be pleasing to You and bring honor to Your name." I prayed what I wanted God to do in my own life.

Within a month of praying passionately for him, I cried with a loud voice, "I bless you! I love you in the name of Jesus!" It was a cry from deep within my spirit. I had gone from praying for him for my sake to praying for him for his sake. I believed the healing was totally complete.

HEALING IN CONFRONTATION

A few more weeks passed, and I saw him again. An uncomfortable sensation lingered in my heart. I still fought the urge to be critical.

"You need to go to him, John," my wife encouraged me.

"No, I don't," I assured her. "I am healed now."

But I sensed that the Holy Spirit did not bear witness with what I had just said. So I asked the Lord if I needed to go to him. He said yes.

I made an appointment with the man and brought him a gift. I humbled myself, confessed my wrong attitude, and asked his forgiveness. We were reconciled, and forgiveness and healing flowed into my heart.

I walked out of his office healed and strengthened. I no longer had to fight the pain, nor was I critical of him. Our relationship has been strong since then, and we have never had another problem. In fact, we are very supportive of each other.

"When I first met that man," I told Lisa, "he could do no wrong in my eyes. I saw no faults in him. I loved him because I thought he was perfect. But when I was hurt, it was hard to love him. It took every bit of faith I had. Now that I have gone through this restoration process and have been healed, I love him with the same intensity as when I first met him, in spite of any faults. It's a mature love."

This Scripture verse came to mind:

And above all things have fervent love for one another, for "love will cover a multitude of sins."

—1 Peter 4:8

It is easy to love those who can do no wrong in our eyes. That's honeymoon love. It is another thing to love someone when we can see their faults, especially when we've been the victim of them. The love of God was maturing me, strengthening my heart.

Since then, similar cases have come up, but it has taken no time at all to release the offense. The reason: My heart was exercised to stay free from offense.

Several months went by from the time God spoke to me in my backyard until I walked out of the man's office healed. That was a training period in which my heart was exercised and strengthened. During those months I seemed at times to be getting nowhere. In fact, I wondered if I had grown worse.

But I was on the sure road to recovery. The Spirit of the Lord led me at a pace I could handle. It was part of my maturing process. I would not trade that experience and am thankful for the growth it brought to my life.

MATURING THROUGH HARDSHIPS

We grow in the tough times, not the easy times. Hard places will always come in our journey with the Lord. We cannot escape them but need to face them, for they are part of the process of becoming perfect in Him. If you choose to run from them, you will seriously hinder your growth.

As you overcome different obstacles, you will be stronger and more compassionate. You will fall more in love with Jesus. If you have come out of hardships and do not feel this way, you have probably not recovered from the offense. Recovery is your choice. Some people get hurt and never recover. As cruel as this may sound, it was their choice.

Jesus learned obedience by the things He suffered. Peter learned obedience by the things he suffered. Paul learned obedience by the things he suffered. What about you? Have you learned? Or are you hard, calloused, cold, bitter, and resentful? Then you did not learn obedience.

Yes, it's true that there are some offenses that will not go away like "water off a duck's back." You will have to work through them, striving to get free. But in that process you will grow and mature.

Maturity does not come easily. If it did, all would attain it. Few reach this level of life because of the resistance they face. There's resistance because the course of our society is not godly but selfish. The world is dominated by the "prince of the power of the air" (Eph. 2:2). As a result, to enter into the maturity of Christ there will be hardships that come from standing against the flow of selfishness.

Paul had returned to three cities where he birthed churches. His purpose was to strengthen the souls of the disciples. However, it is interesting to see how he strengthened them. He encouraged them by:

> ...exhorting them to continue in the faith, and saying, "We must through many tribulations enter the kingdom of God."
>
> —ACTS 14:22

He did not promise them a life of ease. He did not promise them success according to the world's standards. He showed them that if they were going to finish their course with joy, they were going to meet up with much resistance that he called tribulation.

If you are rowing on a river against the current, you will have to row continuously in order to progress against the flow of the river. If you stop rowing and relax, you will eventually flow with the current. Even so, when we are determined to go God's way we will meet up with many tribulations. The trials will all show the answer to one main question: Are you going to look out for yourself as the world does, or are you going to live a self-denied life?

Remember that when we lose our life for the sake of Jesus, we will find His life. Learn to fix your focus on the end result, not the struggle.

Peter put it so well:

> Beloved, do not think it strange concerning the fiery trial which is to try you, as though some strange thing happened to you; but rejoice to the extent that you partake of Christ's sufferings, that when His glory is revealed, you may also be glad with exceeding joy.
>
> —1 PETER 4:12–13

Notice that he compares the extent of suffering to the extent of rejoicing. How can you rejoice to that extent? When His glory is revealed, you will be glorified with Him. This glorifying is to the degree that you allow Him to perfect His character within you. So don't look at the offense. Look at the coming glory. Hallelujah!

IT IS MORE
IMPORTANT TO HELP
A STUMBLING BROTHER THAN
TO PROVE YOURSELF
CORRECT.

I am eighteen years old. I come from a single-parent home with an identical twin sister and a wonderful extended family. I have never met my biological father and have held unforgiveness toward him for all of my life. My grandfather, an awesome man of God, gave me *The Bait of Satan* to read. After reading it, I was able to completely forgive my father.

—N. M., NEW MEXICO

CHAPTER 14

OBJECTIVE: RECONCILIATION

*You have heard that it was said to those of old, "You shall
not murder, and whoever murders will be in danger of
the judgment." But I say to you that whoever is angry
with his brother without a cause shall be in danger of
the judgment. And whoever says to his brother, "Raca!"
shall be in danger of the council. But whoever says, "You
fool!" shall be in danger of hell fire. Therefore if you
bring your gift to the altar, and there remember that your
brother has something against you, leave your gift there
before the altar, and go your way. First be reconciled
to your brother, and then come and offer your gift.*
—MATTHEW 5:21–24

THIS QUOTE COMES FROM THE SERMON ON THE MOUNT. JESUS
started by saying, "You have heard that it was said to those of
old…" Then He said, "But I say to you…"

Jesus continues this comparison throughout this portion of His
message. First He quotes the law that regulates our outward actions.
Then He shows its fulfillment by bringing it into the heart. So in
God's eyes a murderer is not limited to the one who commits murder;
he is also the one who hates his brother. What you are in your heart
is how you really are!

Jesus clearly delineates the consequences of offense in this portion of His sermon. He illustrates the severity of holding anger or bitter offense. If one is angry with his brother without a cause, he is in danger of judgment. He is in danger of the council if that anger bears fruit and he calls his brother "Raca!"[1]

The word *raca* means "empty-headed," or fool. It was a term of reproach used among the Jews in the time of Christ. If that anger reaches the point where he calls a brother a fool, he is in danger of hell. The word *fool* means to be godless.[2] The fool says in his heart there is no God. (See Psalm 14:1.) In those days to call a brother a fool was quite a serious accusation. No one would say such a thing unless the anger they bore had turned to hatred. Today it would be comparable to telling a brother, "Go to hell," and meaning it.

Jesus was showing them that not dealing with anger can lead to hatred. Hatred not dealt with would put them in danger of hell. Then He said that if they remembered their brother was offended with them, they were to make it top priority to find him and seek to be reconciled.

Why should we seek with such urgency to be reconciled—for our sake or for our brother's sake? We should go for his sake that we might be a catalyst to help him out of the offense. Even if we are not offended with him, the love of God does not let him remain angry without attempting to reach out and restore. We may have done nothing wrong. Right or wrong doesn't matter. It is more important for us to help this stumbling brother than to prove ourselves correct.

There are limitless scenarios for offense.

Maybe the person we have offended believes we were unjust in our treatment of him, when in reality we did him no harm. He may have inaccurate information that has yielded an inaccurate conclusion.

On the other hand, he may have *accurate* information from which he has drawn an inaccurate conclusion. What we said may have been grossly distorted once it was processed through the various channels of communication. Though our intent was not to harm, our words and actions gave a different appearance.

Often we judge ourselves by our intentions and everyone else by their actions. It is possible to intend one thing while communicating something totally different. Sometimes our true motives are cleverly hidden even from us. We want to believe they are pure. But as we filter them through the Word of God we see them differently.

Finally, maybe we did sin against the person. We were angry or under pressure, and he got the brunt of it. Or maybe this person has constantly and deliberately lashed out at us, and we were responding in kind.

No matter what caused it, this offended person's understanding is darkened, and he has based his judgments on assumptions, hearsay, and appearances, deceiving himself even though he believes he has discerned our true motives. How can we have an accurate judgment without accurate information? We must be sensitive to the fact that he believes with his whole heart that he has been wronged. For whatever reason he feels this way, we must be willing to humble ourselves and apologize.

Jesus is exhorting us to reconcile even if the offense is not our fault. It takes maturity to walk in humility in order to bring reconciliation. But taking the first step is often harder on the one who is hurting. That's why Jesus told the person who caused the offense to "go to him ..."

ASKING FORGIVENESS OF ONE WHO IS OFFENDED

The apostle Paul said:

> Therefore let us pursue the things which make for peace and the things by which one may edify another.
>
> —ROMANS 14:19

This shows us how to approach a person we have offended. If we go with an attitude of frustration we will not promote peace. We will only make it difficult for the one who is hurt. We are to maintain an attitude of pursuing peace through humility at the expense of our pride. It is the only way to see true reconciliation.

On certain occasions I have approached people I have hurt or who were angry with me, and they have lashed out at me. I have been told I was selfish, inconsiderate, proud, rude, harsh, and more.

My natural response has been to say, "No, I'm not. You just don't understand me!" But when I defend myself, it only fuels their fire of offense. This is not pursuing peace. Standing up for ourselves and "our rights" will never bring true peace.

Instead I have learned to listen and keep my mouth shut until they have said what they need to say. If I don't agree, I let them know I respect what they have said and will search my attitude and intentions. Then I tell them I am sorry I have hurt them.

Other times they are accurate in their assessment of me. I admit, "You are right. I ask your forgiveness."

Once again it simply means humbling ourselves to promote reconciliation. Perhaps this was why Jesus said in the next verses:

> Agree with your adversary quickly, while you are on the way with him, lest your adversary deliver you to the judge, the judge hand you over to the officer, and you be thrown into prison. Assuredly, I say to you, you will by no means get out of there till you have paid the last penny.
>
> —MATTHEW 5:25–26

Pride defends. Humility agrees and says, "You are right. I have acted this way. Please forgive me."

> But the wisdom that is from above is first pure, then peaceable, gentle, *willing to yield,* full of mercy and good fruits, without partiality and without hypocrisy.
>
> —JAMES 3:17, EMPHASIS ADDED

Godly wisdom is willing to yield. It is not stiff-necked or stubborn when it comes to personal conflicts. A person submitted to godly wisdom is not afraid to yield or defer to the other person's viewpoint as long as it does not violate truth.

APPROACHING SOMEONE WHO HAS OFFENDED YOU

Now that we have discussed what to do when we offend our brother, let's consider what to do if our brother offends us.

> Moreover if your brother sins against you, go and tell him his fault between you and him alone. If he hears you, you have gained your brother.
>
> —MATTHEW 18:15

Many people apply this Scripture verse in a different attitude from the one Jesus was intending. If they have been hurt, they will go and confront the offender in a spirit of revenge and anger. They use this verse as justification to condemn the one who has hurt them.

But they are missing the whole reason Jesus instructed us to go to one another. It is not for condemnation but for reconciliation. He does not want us to tell our brother how rotten he has been to us. We are to go to remove the breach preventing the restoration of our relationship.

This parallels how God restores us to Himself. We have sinned against God, but He "demonstrates His own love toward [and for] us, in that while we were still sinners, Christ died for us" (Rom. 5:8). Are we willing to lay down our self-protection and die to pride in order to be restored to the one who has offended us? God reached out to us before we asked for forgiveness. Jesus decided to forgive us before we even acknowledged our offense.

Even though He reached out to us, we could not be reconciled to the Father until we received His word of reconciliation.

> Now all things are of God, who has *reconciled* us to Himself through Jesus Christ, and has given us the ministry of *reconciliation,* that is, that God was in Christ reconciling the world to Himself, not imputing their trespasses to them, and has committed to us the *word of reconciliation.* Now then, we are ambassadors for Christ, as though God were pleading through us: *we implore you on Christ's behalf, be reconciled to God.*
>
> —2 CORINTHIANS 5:18–20, EMPHASIS ADDED

The word of reconciliation begins on the common ground that we all have sinned against God. We do not desire reconciliation or salvation unless we know there is a separation.

In the New Testament, the disciples preached that the people had sinned against God. But why tell people they have sinned? To condemn them? God does not condemn. "For God did not send His Son into the world to condemn the world, but that the world through Him might be saved" (John 3:17). Is it rather to bring them to a place where they realize their condition, repent of their sins, and ask forgiveness?

What leads men to repentance? The answer is found in Romans 2:4.

Or do you despise the riches of His goodness, forbearance, and longsuffering, not knowing that *the goodness of God leads you to repentance?*

—EMPHASIS ADDED

God's goodness leads us to repent. His love does not leave us condemned to hell. He proved His love by sending Jesus, His only Son, to the cross to die for us. God reaches out first, even though we have sinned against Him. He reaches out not to condemn but to restore—to save.

Since we are to imitate God (see Ephesians 5:1), we are to extend reconciliation to a brother who sins against us. Jesus established this pattern: Go to him and show him his sin, not to condemn him but to remove anything that lies between the two of you and thus be reconciled and restored. The goodness of God within us will draw our brother to repentance and restoration of the relationship.

I, therefore, the prisoner of the Lord, beseech you to walk worthy of the calling with which you were called, with all lowliness and gentleness, with longsuffering, bearing with one another in love, endeavoring to keep the unity of the Spirit in the bond of peace.

—EPHESIANS 4:1–3

We keep this bond of peace by maintaining an attitude of humility, gentleness, and long-suffering and by undergirding each other's weakness in love. The bonds of love are strengthened thereby.

I have wronged people who have confronted me with condemnation. As a result I lost all desire to be reconciled. In fact, I thought they didn't want reconciliation; they just wanted me to know they were mad.

Others I have wronged have come to me in meekness. Then I was quick to change my outlook and ask forgiveness—sometimes before they had finished speaking.

Has someone ever come to you and said, "I just want you to know that I forgive you for not being a better friend and for not doing this or that for me"?

Then when they have blasted you, they give you a look that says, "You owe me an apology."

You are baffled and stand there in confusion and hurt. They did not come to reconcile your relationship but to intimidate and control you.

We should not go to a brother who has offended us until we have decided to forgive him from our hearts—no matter how he responds to us. We need to get rid of any feelings of animosity toward him before approaching him. If we don't, we will probably react out of these negative feelings and hurt him, not heal him.

What happens if we have the right attitude and attempt to reconcile with someone who has sinned against us, but he or she won't listen?

> But if he will not hear, take with you one or two more, that "by the mouth of two or three witnesses every word may be established." And if he refuses to hear them, tell it to the church. But if he refuses even to hear the church, let him be to you like a heathen and a tax collector.
>
> —MATTHEW 18:16–17

Each of these progressions has the same goal: reconciliation. In essence Jesus was saying, "Keep trying." Notice how the one who caused the offense is involved at every step. How often we take offenses to everyone else before we go to the one who sinned against us, as Jesus told us to do! We do this because we have not dealt with our own hearts. We feel justified as we tell everyone our side of the story. It strengthens our cause and comforts us when others agree with how badly we have been treated. There is only selfishness in this type of behavior.

THE BOTTOM LINE

If we keep the love of God as our motivation, we will not fail. Love never fails. When we love others the way Jesus loves us, we will be free even if the other person chooses not to be reconciled to us. Look carefully at the following Scripture verse. God's wisdom is available for all situations.

> If it is possible, as much as depends on you, live peaceably with all men.
>
> —ROMANS 12:18

He says, "If it is possible," because there are times when others will refuse to be at peace with us. Or there may be those whose conditions for reconciliation would compromise our relationship with the Lord. In either case it is not possible to restore that relationship.

Notice that God says, "…as much as depends on you." We are to do everything we can to be reconciled with the other person, as long as we remain loyal to truth. We often give up on relationships too soon.

I will never forget the time when a friend counseled me not to walk away from a very frustrating situation. "John, I know you can find scriptural reasons for walking away. Before you do that, make sure you have fought this in prayer and done all you can to bring the peace of God into this situation."

Then he added, "You will regret it if you look back one day and ask yourself if you did all you could to save this relationship. It is better to know that you have no other recourse and that you did as much as possible without compromising truth."

I was very grateful for his counsel and recognized it as the wisdom of God.

Remember Jesus's words:

> Blessed are the peacemakers, for they shall be called sons of God.
>
> —MATTHEW 5:9

He did not say, "Blessed are the peacekeepers." A peacekeeper avoids confrontation at all costs to maintain peace, even at the risk of compromising truth. But the peace he maintains is not true peace. It is a touchy, superficial peace that will not last.

A peacemaker will go in love and confront, bringing truth so that the resulting reconciliation will endure. He will not maintain an artificial, superficial relationship. He desires openness, truth, and love. He refuses to hide offense with a political smile. He makes peace with a bold love that cannot fail.

God is this way with mankind. He is not willing that any should perish. But He will not compromise truth for a relationship. He seeks reconciliation with true commitment, not on superficial terms. This develops a bond of love that no evil can sever. He has laid His life down for us. We can only do likewise.

Remember that the bottom line is the love of God. It never fails, never fades, and never comes to an end. It seeks not its own. It is not easily offended (1 Cor. 13:5).

The apostle Paul wrote that love would overcome all kinds of sin.

> And this I pray, that *your love may abound still more and more* in knowledge and all discernment, that you may approve the things that are excellent, that you may be sincere and *without offense* till the day of Christ, being filled with the fruits of righteousness which are by Jesus Christ, to the glory and praise of God.
> —PHILIPPIANS 1:9–11, EMPHASIS ADDED

The love of God is the key to freedom from the baited trap of offense. This must be an abounding love, a love that continually grows and is strengthened in our hearts.

So many in our society today are deceived by a superficial love, a love that talks but does not act. The love that will keep us from stumbling lays down its life selflessly—even for the good of an enemy. When we walk in this kind of love, we cannot be seduced into taking the bait of Satan.

TAKING ACTION

As you have read this book, the Spirit of the Lord may have reminded you of relationships in the past or present in which you have held something against others. I have sensed the Lord's instruction to ask you to pray a simple prayer of release with me.

But before praying, ask the Holy Spirit to walk with you through your past, bringing before you any people against whom you have held something. Stay quiet before Him as He shows you who they are. You do not need to hunt for something that is not there. He will clearly bring them up to where you will not doubt it. As He does, you may remember the pain you experienced. Don't be afraid. He will be right there at your side comforting you.

As you release these people from blame for what they have done to you, picture each of them individually. Forgive each one personally. Cancel the debt they owe you. Then pray this prayer, but don't be limited to these words. Use this prayer as a guideline, and be led by the Spirit of God.

> *Father, in the name of Jesus, I acknowledge that I have sinned against You by not forgiving those who have offended me. I repent of this and ask Your forgiveness.*
>
> *I also acknowledge my inability to forgive them apart from You. Therefore, from my heart I choose to forgive* [insert their names—release each one individually]. *I bring under the blood of Jesus all that they have done wrong to me. They no longer owe me anything. I remit their sins against me.*

Heavenly Father, as my Lord Jesus asked You to forgive those who had sinned against Him, I pray that Your forgiveness will come to those who have sinned against me.

I ask that You will bless them and lead them into a closer relationship with You. Amen.

Now write the names of the people you have released in a journal, and record that on this date you made the decision to forgive them.

You may have to exercise to stay free from offense. (Reread chapter 13 if you don't understand this statement.) Make a commitment to pray for them as you would pray for yourself. The journal will help you remember. If thoughts continue to bombard your mind, cast them down with the Word of God and declare your decision to forgive. You have asked for God's grace to forgive, and unforgiveness is not as powerful as His grace. Be bold and fight the good fight of faith.

When you know your heart is strong and settled, go to them. Remember that you are going for the purpose of reconciliation for their benefit, not your own. By doing this you will seal the victory. You will win a brother. (See Matthew 18:15.) This is well pleasing in the sight of God.

Now to Him who is able to keep you from stumbling, and to present you faultless before the presence of His glory with exceeding joy, to God our Savior, who alone is wise, be glory and majesty, dominion and power, both now and forever. Amen.

—JUDE 24–25

NOTES

CHAPTER ONE
ME, OFFENDED?

1. W. E. Vine, Merrill Unger, and William White Jr., *An Expository Dictionary of Biblical Words* (Nashville, TN: Thomas Nelson, 1984), s.v. "offence, offend" (hereafter cited as *Vine's Expository Dictionary*).

CHAPTER SIX
HIDING FROM REALITY

1. *Vine's Expository Dictionary*, s.v. "child."
2. *Vine's Expository Dictionary*, s.v. "son."
3. Under the entry for "son" in *Vine's Expository Dictionary of New Testament Words* (unabridged edition), the author made these powerful statements about the difference between a child by birth (*teknon*) and a son by resemblance (*huios*):

   "The difference between believers as 'children of God' *teknon* and as 'sons of God' *huios* is brought out in Romans 8:14–21. The Spirit bears witness with their spirit that they are 'children of God,' and, as such, they are His heirs and joint-heirs with Christ. This stresses the fact of their spiritual birth (vv. 16–17). On the other hand, 'as many as are led by the Spirit of God, these are sons of God,' i.e., 'these and no other.' Their conduct gives evidence of the dignity of their relationship and their likeness to His character.

   "The Lord Jesus used *huios* in a very significant way, as in 'called the sons of God,' and vv. 44, 45, 'Love your enemies and pray for those who persecute you, that you may be [become] sons of your Father in heaven.' The disciples were to do these things, not in order that they might become children of God, but that, being children (note 'your Father' throughout), they might make the fact manifest in their character, might 'become sons.' See also 2 Corinthians 6:17–18."
4. The Rockford Institute, Center on the Family in America (Rockford, IL).

CHAPTER SEVEN
THE SURE FOUNDATION

1. *Zondervan Topical Bible* (Grand Rapids, MI: Zondervan, 1969), s.v. "Simon."

2. *Vine's Expository Dictionary,* s.v. "rock."
3. Ibid.

CHAPTER EIGHT
ALL THAT CAN BE SHAKEN WILL BE SHAKEN

1. Logos Bible Study Software for Microsoft, version 1.6 (Oak Harbor, WA: Logos Research Systems Inc., 1993), s.v. "sift."
2. J. D. Douglas, et al., eds., *New Bible Dictionary* (Wheaton, IL: Tyndale House, 1982), 2nd ed., s.v. "Peter."

CHAPTER ELEVEN
FORGIVENESS: YOU DON'T GIVE—YOU DON'T GET

1. Margin note: New King James Version (Nashville, TN: Thomas Nelson, 1988).
2. Logos Bible Study Software, version 1.6 (Oak Harbor, WA: Logos Research Systems Inc., 1993).
3. *Merriam-Webster's Collegiate Dictionary,* Tenth Edition (Springfield, MA: Merriam-Webster Inc., 1993).

CHAPTER TWELVE
REVENGE: THE TRAP

1. Francis Frangipane, *The Three Battlegrounds* (Cedar Rapids, IA: Advancing Church Publications, 1989), 50.

CHAPTER THIRTEEN
ESCAPING THE TRAP

1. *Vine's Expository Dictionary,* s.v. "exercise."

CHAPTER FOURTEEN
OBJECTIVE: RECONCILIATION

1. *Vine's Expository Dictionary,* s.v. "raca."
2. Ibid.

THE BAIT OF SATAN

CONTENTS

INTRODUCTION

WELCOME TO THIS DEVOTIONAL SUPPLEMENT, WHICH IS A PART of the tenth anniversary edition of John Bevere's book *The Bait of Satan*. This devotional guide is written for you to use in your devotional time. It will help you to probe more deeply into Bible truths related to the book, enabling you to resist taking up offense, and to repent of and get rid of offenses that may have impacted you in the past. We want to help you discover God's plan for handling offenses.

Each daily devotional segment is structured to:

- Help you to encounter God's Word
- Provide you with assigned reading from *The Bait of Satan*
- Reveal life-giving principles for developing healthy, loving, and offense-free relationships
- Aid you in being set free from the bondage of past offenses

We pray that this devotional supplement will be an effective tool for equipping you to discover God's truths for resisting the bait of Satan—offenses—in your relationships with God, self, family, church, friends, work associates, and even those who think of themselves as your enemies.

DAY 1

ME, OFFENDED?

And a servant of the Lord must not quarrel but be gentle to all, able to teach, patient, in humility correcting those **who are in opposition,** *if God perhaps will grant them repentance, so that they may know the truth, and that they may come to their senses and escape the snare [entrapment] of the devil, having been taken captive by him to do his will.*
—2 TIMOTHY 2:24–26, EMPHASIS ADDED

[Read chapter 1, stopping at the heading "The Heart's True Condition."]

ANYONE WHO HAS TRAPPED ANIMALS KNOWS THAT A TRAP needs two things to be successful: It must be hidden in the hope that an animal will stumble upon it, and it must be baited to lure the animal into the trap's deadly jaws.

Many people are unable to function properly in God's purpose and calling for their lives because of the wounds, hurts, and offenses in their lives.

Satan, the enemy of our souls, incorporates both of these strategies as he lays out his most deceptive and deadly traps. They are both hidden and baited. Along with his cohorts, Satan is not as blatant as many believe. He is subtle and delights in deception. He is shrewd in his operation, cunning and crafty.

One of his most deceptive and insidious kinds of bait is something every Christian has encountered—offense. But if we pick it up, consume it, and feed on it in our hearts, then we become offended.

Offended people produce much fruit.

In the following list of the fruit of offense, circle the feelings you have experienced when offended in the past:

Hurt	Anger	Outrage
Jealousy	Envy	Resentment
Strife	Bitterness	Hatred

Many people are unable to function properly in God's purpose and calling for their lives because of the wounds, hurts, and offenses in their lives. They are handicapped and hindered from fulfilling their potential. Most often, hurt from a fellow believer causes them to say with David, "For it is not an enemy who reproaches me; then I could bear it. Nor is it one who hates me who has exalted himself against me; then I could hide from him. But it was you, a man my equal, my companion and my acquaintance. We took sweet counsel together, and walked to the house of God in the throng" (Ps. 55:12–14).

List (with 1 being the closest, and 5 being the most distant relationship) the names of five people who have offended you:

1. _____
2. _____
3. _____
4. _____
5. _____

Offended people hurt, and their understanding is darkened. They begin to judge others by assumption, appearance, and hearsay. In this devotional supplement, we will uncover God's way to avoid Satan's bait of offense and overcome any past offenses that still bind us.

WRITE A PRAYER...

Asking God for His help and wisdom to avoid the bait of Satan.

_____

_____

_____

_____

DAY 2

THE HEART'S
TRUE CONDITION

*In this you greatly rejoice, though now for a little while, if
need be, you have been grieved by various trials, that the
genuineness of your faith, being much more precious than
gold that perishes, though it is tested by fire, may be found
to praise, honor, and glory at the revelation of Jesus Christ.*
—1 Peter 1:6–7

*[Read the remainder of chapter 1, beginning with the heading "The
Heart's True Condition."]*

ONE WAY THE ENEMY KEEPS A PERSON IN AN OFFENDED STATE IS
to keep the offense hidden and cloaked with pride.

Pride will keep you from admitting your true condition. Pride causes
you to view yourself as a victim. Because you believe you were treated
unjustly, you hold back forgiveness. Though your heart's true condition is
hidden from you, it is not hidden from God. Being mistreated does not
give you permission to hold on to an offense. Two wrongs do not make
a right.

Pure gold is refined in fire (Rev. 3:18). When gold is mixed with
other metals, it becomes hard, less pliable, and more corrosive. As it

goes through the fire, the other metals (dross) are burned away, and the gold becomes pure and pliable.

Being mistreated does not give you permission to hold on to an offense. Two wrongs do not make a right.

The same is true of our hearts. The more our hearts are hardened by pride and sin as we hold on to offenses, the more resistant to God we become. God desires to purify our hearts.

Read 1 Peter 1:6–7, and then summarize how God purifies us:

_____

_____

_____

God refines us with afflictions, trials, and tribulations, the heat of which separates impurities such as unforgiveness, anger, envy, and jealousy, and allows the character of God (purity and holiness) to grow in our lives.

Think about your own life. What are the impurities in your heart that are hindering the character of God from growing in your life?

_____

_____

_____

Jesus said that our ability to see correctly is a key to being freed from deception. Often when we are offended, we see ourselves as victims and blame those who have hurt us. We justify all the negative feelings we have as they surface. Sometimes we even resent those who remind us of others who have hurt us. Jesus counseled, "Anoint your eyes with eye salve, that you may see" (Rev. 3:18).

WRITE A PRAYER...

Repenting of blaming others and asking the Lord to give you eyes to see the condition of your heart.

_____

_____

_____

Day 3

MASSIVE OFFENSE

*For he who sows to his flesh will of the flesh reap corruption,
but he who sows to the Spirit will of the Spirit reap
everlasting life. And let us not grow weary while doing
good, for in due season we shall reap if we do not lose heart.*
—Galatians 6:8–9

[Read chapter 2, stopping at the heading "Walls of Protection."]

MOST AGREE THE RETURN OF JESUS WILL BE SOON. IT IS USELESS to try to pinpoint the actual day of His return. Only the Father knows that. But Jesus said we would know the season, and it is now! Never before have we seen such prophetic fulfillment in the church, in Israel, and in nature. Jesus said that one of the signs of His return was that "many will be offended"—not a few, not some, but many. Are you or the people you know easily offended?

I have come to realize that whenever I give love, I am sowing to the Spirit and will eventually reap a harvest of love.

Put an x on the line to indicate your level of offense for each statement:

Church people seem to be easily offended.

_____

USUALLY TRUE   SELDOM TRUE

I offend easily.

_____

USUALLY TRUE   SELDOM TRUE

Friends seem to offend easily.

_____

USUALLY TRUE   SELDOM TRUE

People at work get offended easily.

_____

USUALLY TRUE   SELDOM TRUE

Relatives get easily offended.

_____

USUALLY TRUE   SELDOM TRUE

If you found yourself putting *x*'s more often to the left of center, then you too are observing how easily people seem to get offended in this season. But a believer, filled with God's love, sows His love and refuses to take the bait of offense.

I have come to realize that whenever I give love, I am sowing to the Spirit and will eventually reap a harvest of love. I did not always know where love would be manifested, but I knew the harvest would come. No longer did I perceive failure when love was not returned from the person I was loving. I was freed up to love that person even more.

If we walk in a selfish love—expecting others to meet our expectations for love—then we will be easily offended when they don't respond as we desire. I set myself up for offense when I require certain behaviors and attitudes from those whom I love. The more I expect, the greater the potential offense.

On a scale of 1 (very little) to 5 (very much), how would you rate each of the following statements in your own life: (Circle your answers.)

I expect much of others.	1	2	3	4	5
I am easily disappointed.	1	2	3	4	5
I love conditionally.	1	2	3	4	5
I bless to be blessed.	1	2	3	4	5

Add together all the numbers you circled. If you scored over ten, you are positioning yourself for potential offenses in your life.

WRITE A PRAYER...

Asking God to replace your expectations of others with unconditional love for them.

_____

_____

_____

DAY 4

WALLS OF PROTECTION

For the weapons of our warfare are not carnal but mighty in God for pulling down strongholds, casting down arguments and every high thing that exalts itself against the knowledge of God, bringing every thought into captivity to the obedience of Christ.
—2 CORINTHIANS 10:4–5

[Read the remainder of chapter 2, beginning with the heading "Walls of Protection."]

AN OFFENDED PERSON IS HARDER TO WIN THAN A FORTIFIED city with a strong wall around it. The walls were the city's assurance of protection. They kept out unwelcome inhabitants and invaders.

We must come to the place where we trust God— not our flesh—to protect us from offense.

We often construct walls around ourselves when we are hurt in order to safeguard our hearts and prevent future wounds.

Check ✔ any attitudes you find in yourself: From within our walls we become…

❑ Selective about relationships

❑ Less open and vulnerable to others
❑ Closed to those we fear will hurt us
❑ Reticent to admit those who owe us something
❑ Open only to those who we believe are on our side

In an attempt to protect ourselves from offense, we find ourselves imprisoned within our walls, unable to relate deeply to those around us. Our focus is turned inward and introspective. We guard our rights and personal relationships carefully. Our energy is consumed with making sure no future injuries will occur. Yet if we cannot risk being hurt, we cannot give unconditional love. Unconditional love gives others the right to hurt us.

Complete the following lists, listing both those who have the right to hurt you and those you have shut out with walls.

Those who can hurt me:

_____

_____

_____

Those I have walled out:

_____

_____

_____

Offended people who build walls will always be able to find Scripture passages to support their position and to keep others away, but their interpretations do not correctly divide the Word of God. The knowledge of God's Word, without love, is a destructive force—it puffs us up with pride and legalism (1 Cor. 8:1–3). It causes us to justify ourselves rather than repent of unforgiveness.

Knowledge without the love of God will lead to deception—especially from false prophets. Jesus warns us, "Then many false prophets will rise up and deceive many" (Matt. 24:11). The ones whom they deceive are those who dwell inside high walls where love has grown cold (v. 12).

Seeking our own protection or benefit at the expense of someone else—betrayal—occurs in the church between believers. Betrayal is the ultimate abandonment of covenant. When betrayal occurs, the relationship cannot be restored unless genuine repentance follows.

We must come to the place where we trust God—not our flesh—to protect us from offense. The sin of offense is serious. If it is not dealt with, offense will eventually lead to death. But when you resist the temptation to build walls of offense, God brings great victory.

WRITE A PRAYER...

Asking God to help you tear down your walls, become vulnerable, and repent of any offenses.

_____

_____

_____

DAY 5

HOW COULD
THIS HAPPEN TO ME?

Joseph said to them ... "But as for you, you meant
evil against me; but God meant it for good."
—GENESIS 50:19–20

[Read chapter 3, stopping at the subheading "Is God in control?"]

ALL OFFENDED PEOPLE FALL INTO TWO CATEGORIES: THOSE WHO
have been genuinely mistreated, and those who think they have
been mistreated but actually were not.

When you have been genuinely mistreated, do you have the right
to be offended? Reflect for a few minutes on a time when someone
hurt you intentionally. What was your response? Did you become
offended at that person because of the hurt? Was that your normal
response to offense?

From the following list, rank your normal responses to offense from 1
(most likely response) to 5 (least likely response):

_____ I get mad.
_____ I immediately forgive.
_____ I get even.
_____ I work hard at forgiving the person.

_____   I get away from the person.

_____   I seek to be reconciled.

If the negative responses above are the ones you ranked the highest, then you actually feel you have the right to be offended when someone hurts you. But you do not have to respond that way.

Consider the story of Joseph. (Read Genesis 37–48.) How do you evaluate Joseph's words and actions?

Put an x on each line to indicate how Joseph responded.

HE BECAME OFFENDED.   HE FORGAVE.

HE BLAMED OTHERS FOR HIS CIRCUMSTANCES.   HE TRUSTED GOD.

HE SOUGHT REVENGE.   HE SOUGHT TO BE RECONCILED.

If you had been Joseph, how would you have responded? Would you have believed that you had the right to be offended?

Satan hopes we will take his bait of offense so that he will have a foothold into our lives.

If the devil could destroy us whenever he wanted to, he would have wiped us out a long time ago. Satan hopes we will take his bait of offense so that he will have a foothold into our lives to destroy both our relationships with God and our relationships with others. Don't take the bait, and Satan cannot touch you!

WRITE A PRAYER...

Asking God for the wisdom of Joseph to avoid taking offense and to trust Him instead of blaming others or circumstances for difficulties in life.

DAY 6

IS GOD IN CONTROL?

For God sent me before you to preserve life.... And
God sent me before you to preserve a posterity for you in
the earth, and to save your lives by a great deliverance.
So now it was not you who sent me here, but God.
—GENESIS 45:5, 7–8

[Read the remainder of chapter 3, beginning with the subheading "Is
God in control?"]

JOSEPH PROBABLY NEVER THOUGHT ABOUT RULING EGYPT WHILE languishing in prison. But through all the circumstances of his life, Joseph was being prepared by God for His plan. God has a plan for the life of every believer. He is in control. The bottom line for Joseph was his responses to his brothers, to Potiphar, and to his circumstances. He could have blamed his brothers or God for his suffering. It is easy to blame everyone else in life for your problems and imagine how much better off we would be if it were not for all the people around us.

No one but God holds your destiny. No man, woman, child, or devil can ever get you out of the will of God!

No man, woman, child, or devil can ever
get you out of the will of God!

183

Joseph's brothers thought they had killed the dream God had for him, but they couldn't do it. When Joseph was reunited with his brothers, he reminded them not of their wrong but of what God had done for him.

Read Genesis 45:5–8 and Psalm 105:16–17. Jot down all the reasons why God sent Joseph through his trials.

God sent Joseph to _____
(Gen. 45:5).

God sent Joseph to _____
(Gen. 45:7).

God sent Joseph to _____
(Gen. 45:8).

God sent Joseph to _____
(Ps. 105:16–17).

Think of the greatest problem you have faced in the last year. Describe it in one sentence.

_____

_____

Now complete these sentences:

My response to my problem was _____

_____.

God's plan was _____

_____.

What I learned about myself was _____

_____.

If you stay free from offense, you will stay in the will of God. If you become offended, you will be taken captive by the enemy to fulfill his own purpose and will. So take your pick: *Which will it be?*

Stay submitted to God. Resist the devil by not becoming offended. The dream or vision for your life will probably happen differently than you think it will, but His Word and His promises will not fail. Disobedience is the only thing that can abort God's plan.

WRITE A PRAYER...

Thanking God for having a good plan for your life and for working for good all the circumstances of your life.

_____

_____

_____

_____

Day 7

WHEN REJECTED
BY A FATHER

*And he will turn the hearts of the fathers to the
children, and the hearts of the children to their fathers,
lest I come and strike the earth with a curse.*
—Malachi 4:6

[Read chapter 4, stopping at the heading "Who Will Avenge Me?"]

It is one thing to experience rejection and malice from a
brother, but it is entirely different to experience rejection and malice
from a father. When I speak of fathers, I am not just referring to a biological father, but to any leader God puts over us. These are the people
we trusted to love, train, nurture, and care for us.

Think of the "fathers" in the past from whom you have experienced rejection.

Circle any who have rejected or hurt you.

Biological father	Stepfather	Pastor
Church staff	Elder	Deacon
Boss	Teacher	Leader
Close friend who fathered me		

Other: _____

—

One biblical example of a father's rejection was Saul's rejection of David. Carefully read the material under the heading "A Love-Hate Relationship."

As you read, jot down all the ways David could have been tempted to take up an offense against Saul.

_____

_____

Now complete these sentences:

David treated Saul _____.

Instead of revenge, David _____.

When rejected by his king, mentor, and father figure, David chose not to take up an offense. But Saul became jealous and suspicious of his servant David. Today many leaders have become suspicious of individuals under their authority. Like Saul, they are insecure in their calling, and that breeds jealousy and pride. They recognize godly qualities in other people, but they are willing to use such people in ministry only as long as it benefits them. Saul enjoyed the success of David until he saw David's success as a threat to him. Then he demoted David and watched for a reason to destroy him.

If your father figure or leader is doing something sinful and wrong, instead of being offended, pray for that person.

Is there a father in your life who is suspicious of you? If so, what response does God require of you?

Read 1 Samuel 24:11 and then complete these sentences:

When someone attacks me, God wants me to _____

_____

_____.

When someone rejects me, God wants me to _____

_____

_____.

    If your father figure or leader is doing something sinful and wrong, instead of being offended, pray for that person. God will correct him—that's His job, not yours. Refuse to take up an offense.

WRITE A PRAYER...

Asking God to work in the lives of your father figures and to enable you to pray for them and forgive their faults.

_____

_____

_____

_____

DAY 8

WHO WILL AVENGE ME?

Vengeance is Mine, I will repay, says the Lord.
—ROMANS 12:19

[Read the remainder of chapter 4, beginning with the heading "Who Will Avenge Me?"]

SAUL ACKNOWLEDGED DAVID'S GOODNESS WHEN HE REALIZED that David could have killed him and did not. But one of David's men, Abishai, did not possess the grace that David possessed.

When David and Abishai slipped into Saul's camp while he was sleeping, Abishai pleaded with David, "God has delivered your enemy into your hand this day. Now therefore, please, let me strike him at once with the spear right to the earth; and I will not have to strike him a second time!"

Abishai had very good reasons for thinking that David should allow him to kill Saul.

Look over the following list. Check ✔ whether or not you believe that Saul should have received the death penalty for such a crime.

1. Saul had murdered eighty-five innocent priests and their families (multiple counts of first-degree murder).

    ❑ Deserving of death ❑ Allowed to live

2. Saul, along with three thousand men, attempted in every possible way to kill David and his men (multiple counts of attempted murder).

    ❑ Deserving of death ❑ Allowed to live

3. Saul continued to function as king even when the anointing to rule had been taken from him and given to David.

    ❑ Deserving of punishment ❑ Allowed to live

4. Saul lied about David, sought to turn everyone against David, and broke his promises to David.

    ❑ Deserving of punishment ❑ Allowed to live

If these were not good enough reasons for Saul's death, they were at least good enough for punishing Saul and exacting vengeance upon him. Now read David's response to Abishai in 1 Samuel 26:9–11. David would not kill Saul or even seek to punish him, although he had every right in the natural to do so. How many people today would have had a heart like David's?

Any sowing of discord or separation among brethren is an abomination to God.

Churches split, families divide, marriages shatter, and love dies, crushed by an onslaught of words launched in hurt and frustration. Friends, family, and leaders offend us using words sharpened by bitterness and anger that aim a deadly blow. Even though the information may be factual and accurate, often our motives are impure. Any sowing of discord or separation among brethren is an abomination to God (Prov. 6:16–19).

WRITE A PRAYER...

Asking God to teach you to humble yourself before those who offend you and to ask for forgiveness.

_____

_____

_____

_____

_____

DAY 9

HOW SPIRITUAL
VAGABONDS ARE BORN

*"The LORD forbid that I should do this thing to my
master, the LORD's anointed, to stretch out my hand
against him, seeing he is the anointed of the LORD."
So David restrained his servants with these words,
and did not allow them to rise against Saul.*
—1 SAMUEL 24:6–7

[Read chapter 5, stopping at the heading "The Planted Flourish."]

IN THE RELATIONSHIP BETWEEN SAUL AND DAVID, GOD WAS
testing David's heart (1 Sam. 24:6–7). God wanted to see whether
David would kill to establish his kingdom after the order of Saul, or
whether he would allow God to establish His throne forever.

Only God has the right to judge and avenge. In Romans 12:19
we read, "Beloved, do not avenge yourselves, but rather give place
to wrath; for it is written, 'Vengeance is Mine, I will repay,' says the
Lord." We must not take the prerogatives of God into our own hands.
It is wrong to do a right thing in the wrong way.

Yes, Saul deserved to be judged and punished—but by God, not
by David.

Think of a time when you took vengeance into your own hands and did not wait upon God. Describe the situation and its outcome or consequences.

_____

_____

_____

Many people ask, "Why does God put people under leaders who make serious mistakes and even some who are wicked?" (See 1 Samuel 1–5 as an example.) As an innocent child, God put Samuel under the corrupt priesthood of Israel. There Samuel learned to lean upon, trust, and hear directly from God—not man. And God Himself dealt with the corrupt leaders.

God often places us in uncomfortable places and under increasing pressure so that we may be shaped by His love and refining fire. If we take offense and leave, we fail to receive what God has for us; we begin to add offense to offense. Offended people react to the offending situation and do things that appear right even though they are not inspired by God. We are not called to react to people or situations but to act obediently in response to God.

> **God often places us in uncomfortable places and under increasing pressure so that we may be shaped by His love and refining fire.**

Often when we feel pressure, we look for a word from God to bring relief. But God puts us in these very uncomfortable crucibles to mature, refine, and strengthen us—not destroy us!

Give yourself the following test.

1. Do I run from God's refining pressure?
    ❏ Yes   ❏ No

2. Do I complain when under pressure?
    ❏ Yes   ❏ No

3. Do I justify my sin and condemn sin in others?
   ❏ Yes   ❏ No

4. Do I expect spiritual leaders to be perfect when I am not?
   ❏ Yes   ❏ No

5. Am I willing to listen to God and wait on His leading?
   ❏ Yes   ❏ No

6. Read Isaiah 55:12. Am I willing to leave in peace?
   ❏ Yes   ❏ No

WRITE A PRAYER...

Asking Jesus to be your perfect Shepherd and to fill you with His love for the human shepherds He has placed in your life.

_____

_____

_____

DAY 10

THE PLANTED FLOURISH

*Those who are planted in the house of the LORD
shall flourish in the courts of our God. They shall
still bear fruit in old age; they shall be fresh and
flourishing, to declare that the LORD is upright.*
—PSALM 92:13–15

*[Read the remainder of chapter 5, beginning with the heading "The
Planted Flourish."]*

MANY PEOPLE GO FROM CHURCH TO CHURCH, MINISTRY TEAM
to ministry team, trying to develop their ministry. If God puts
them in a place where they are not recognized and encouraged, they
are easily offended. If they don't agree with the way something is done,
they are offended and go somewhere else. Offended people uproot
themselves, complain, blame the leadership, and never realize their
own flaws.

God continues to refine and mature us by increasing pressure in
the areas where we need to grow. If we keep changing the place where
we are planted, we will never grow spiritually the way God intends.

> If we keep changing the place where we are planted,
> we will never grow spiritually the way God intends.

List all the churches to which you have belonged in the last ten years:

_____

_____

_____

If you have changed churches, why? Check ✔ all the reasons you moved.

❏ Moved to another town
❏ Changed denominations
❏ Offended at pastor
❏ Offended at a staff person
❏ Offended by lay leader(s)
❏ Offended by doctrine
❏ Offended by style of worship
❏ Offended by _____
❏ Other reasons: _____

If offense was the reason for changing churches, then you are carrying the bait of Satan from one place to the next, sowing negative seeds and spiritual barrenness wherever you go.

Read the following scriptures, and then jot down what they have to say about the relationship between God's law, offense, spiritual growth, and bearing fruit.

Psalm 1:1–3

_____

_____

_____

Psalm 119:165

_____

_____

_____

Mark 4:16–17

_____

_____

_____

List five benefits that come to you when you refuse to take up an offense and are planted in a church fellowship.

1. _____

2. _____

3. _____

4. _____

5. _____

WRITE A PRAYER...

Thanking God for the church He has planted you in and asking Him to mature and prosper you there.

_____

_____

_____

DAY 11

HIDING FROM REALITY

[They are] always learning and never able
to come to the knowledge of the truth.
—2 TIMOTHY 3:7

[Read chapter 6, stopping at the heading "Self-Preservation."]

I'M OFTEN ASKED BY PEOPLE HOW TO KNOW WHEN IT IS TIME TO leave a church or a ministry team. In turn, I ask them, "Who sent you to your present church?"

Most people respond, "God did." I then explain that if God sent them there, it will not be time to leave until God releases them. When God does instruct you to leave, you will go out with peace, no matter the condition of the ministry (Isa. 55:12).

Describe a time when God released you from a church and allowed you to maintain peaceful relationships since you left.

_____

_____

_____

In this book I have described the difference between *teknon* ("babies or immature sons") and *huois* ("mature sons"). Romans 8:14 speaks of mature sons: "For as many as are led by the Spirit of God, these are sons [*huois*] of God." How does God mature us as His children? In order to understand the process of spiritual maturity we can observe the perfect example of the mature Son of God—Jesus Christ.

Offense blocks spiritual growth, but suffering and obedience take us to a deeper relationship with the Lord and with others.

Jesus matured through obedience and suffering.

What are you learning about suffering and obedience right now in the church in which you find yourself? How are you growing in your attitudes, thoughts, and emotions so as to avoid taking up an offense against others or God when you face suffering or are required to fulfill obedience?

_____

_____

_____

We need to learn that offense blocks spiritual growth, but suffering and obedience take us to a deeper relationship with the Lord and with others.

Complete the following sentences:

When I suffer, I respond _____

_____.

When I must obey, my attitude is _____

_____.

WRITE A PRAYER...

Surrendering all in obedience to God and offering yourself as a vessel willing to suffer for Christ.

_____

_____

_____

_____

Day 12

SELF-PRESERVATION

For the battle is the Lord's, and He
will give you into our hands.
—1 Samuel 17:47

[Read the remainder of chapter 6, beginning with the heading "Self-
Preservation."]

A COMMON EXCUSE FOR SELF-PRESERVATION THROUGH DISOBEDI-
ence is offense. Harboring an offense gives one a false sense of
self-protection. It keeps you from seeing your own character flaws
because the blame is deferred to another. You never have to face your
immaturity or your sin because you see only the faults of the offender.
Therefore God's desire to develop character in you through opposition
is thwarted. The offended person will avoid the source of the offense
and eventually flee, becoming a spiritual vagabond.

The Bible has much to say about judging and blaming others.

Read the following verses and jot down what they say to you about
judging and blaming others.

Matthew 7:1–5

_____

_____

Matthew 5:21–26

_____

_____

_____

Luke 6:36–37

_____

_____

_____

Romans 2:1–2

_____

_____

_____

Romans 12:17–21

_____

_____

_____

Romans 14:10–13

_____

_____

_____

James 4:11–12

_____

_____

_____

Jesus said in John 20:23, "If you forgive the sins of any, they are for-given them; if you retain the sins of any, they are retained."

Love forgets wrongs so that there is hope for the future.

We preserve the sins of other people when we pick up an offense and harbor resentment. The key is to refuse to run from problems, face those who are offensive, and be reconciled. Why? Refusing to deal with an offense will not free us from the problem. The root of the problem remains untouched. God's plan often causes us to face hurts and attitudes we don't want to face. The offenses from which we are tempted to run will bring strength to our lives.

Remember: Love forgets wrongs so that there is hope for the future. If we have truly overcome an offense, we will earnestly seek to make peace. The time may not be right immediately, but in our hearts we will watch for an opportunity for restoration.

WRITE A PRAYER...

Asking for God's help to face offenses and not run from them.

_____

_____

_____

Day 13

THE SURE FOUNDATION

Therefore thus says the Lord God: "Behold, I lay in Zion a stone for a foundation, a tried stone, a precious cornerstone, a sure foundation; whoever believes will not act hastily."
—Isaiah 28:16

[Read chapter 7, stopping at the heading "No Other Option."]

WHOEVER BELIEVES WILL NOT ACT HASTILY. A PERSON WHO acts hastily is an unstable person because his actions are not properly founded. This person is easily moved and swayed by the storms of persecutions and trials.

The only sure foundation in the midst of persecution and trials is the Word of God. When I preach, I have often admonished congregations and individuals to listen for God's voice within my voice. When we listen to an anointed minister speak, or as we read a book, we should look for the words or phrases that explode in our spirit. This is the word God is revealing to us. It conveys light and spiritual understanding.

The psalmist said, "The entrance of Your words gives light; it gives understanding to the simple" (Ps. 119:130). It is the entrance of His Word into our hearts, not minds, that illuminates and clarifies.

How does the Word illuminate your life weekly? Check ✔ each of the following ways you hear God's voice for your life.

- ❏ Bible study
- ❏ Singing Scripture
- ❏ Teaching
- ❏ Listening to Scripture choruses
- ❏ Other _____

- ❏ Bible reading
- ❏ Preaching
- ❏ Reading Christian books

What God reveals by His Spirit cannot be taken from us. We root our decisions in His Word. Without a foundation in His Word, we will be easily offended by unexpected trials and tribulations. When God's Word is not rooted in us, we may receive it with gladness at first but later become offended (Mark 4:16–17).

Without a foundation in His Word, we will be easily offended by unexpected trials and tribulations.

When you hear a word from God that contradicts a feeling, thought, or behavior what is your immediate response? Prioritize from most often (1), to least often (7).

- _____ I get angry.
- _____ I am confused.
- _____ I feel hurt.
- _____ I repent.
- _____ I rejoice in learning what God is saying.
- _____ I get offended.
- _____ I blame others or God.
- _____ Other

Being rooted in God's Word and illuminated by His Spirit will enable us to hear truth from God and from others without becoming offended.

WRITE A PRAYER...

Thanking God for His Word and for the many ways to illuminate it for your life.

_____

_____

_____

DAY 14

YOU HAVE NO
OTHER OPTION THAN...

*Coming to Him as to a living stone, rejected indeed by men,
but chosen by God and precious, you also, as living stones, are
being built up a spiritual house, a holy priesthood, to offer up
spiritual sacrifices acceptable to God through Jesus Christ.*
—1 PETER 2:4–5

*[Read the remainder of chapter 7, beginning with the heading "No
Other Option."]*

THE REVEALED WORD OF GOD IS THE SOLID ROCK ON WHICH WE
are to build our lives and ministries. Its commands and laws are
not optional; they are mandatory. Just because a command or law in the
Word might be offensive, we do not have the options of offense and
disobedience. The only option we have is to obey.

*Describe a time in your life when you took offense at the Word and did
not obey. What were the consequences?*

_____

_____

_____

In the midst of trials and pressures, we find ourselves, like Peter, becoming as stones—little rocks being built into spiritual houses. Peter (*Petra*) is a rock, a stone confessing that Jesus Christ is the Son of the living God.

Trials and testings locate a person. In other words, they determine your spiritual position. They reveal the true condition of your heart.

The Bible refers to a house built on the sand (Matt. 7:26–27). Such a house may be five stories tall and decorated beautifully. As long as the sun is shining, the house looks like a bulwark of strength and beauty. Next to that house may be a plain, single-story house that is almost unnoticeable and unattractive in comparison to the beautiful edifice next to it. But it is built on something you can't see—rock.

Trials and testings locate a person. In other words, they determine your spiritual position.

As long as no storms strike, the five-story house looks much nicer. But when it encounters a severe storm, the five-story house will collapse in ruins. Christians are living stones whose houses are built on the rock of Jesus Christ. When storms come, they do not run, take offense, or blame others. Rather, in the storms of life, they stand firm.

Have you attempted to build a house on the sandy foundations of this world's system? Check ✔ *any of the worldly foundations listed below that you have been tempted to use. Briefly describe the result:*

❏ Money: _____

❏ Success: _____

❏ Power: _____

❏ Possessions: _____

❏ Security: _____

❏ People: _____

❏ Other: _____

Be sure that you build your life on God's revealed Word, not on what others do or say. Keep seeking the Lord and listening to His voice as He speaks to your heart. Don't do or say things just to please everyone else. Seek Him, and stand on what is illuminated in your heart!

WRITE A PRAYER...

Asking God's Spirit to reveal His Word to you and to help you to build your life upon the Rock of Christ.

_____

_____

_____

DAY 15

ALL THAT CAN BE
SHAKEN WILL BE SHAKEN

He has promised, saying, "Yet once more I shake not only the earth, but also heaven." Now this, "Yet once more," indicates the removal of those things that are being shaken, as of things that are made, that the things which cannot be shaken may remain.
—HEBREWS 12:26–27

[Read chapter 8, stopping at the heading "Grace Is Given to the Humble."]

EVEN THOUGH SIMON PETER WAS NAMED "ROCK" AND CONFESSED Jesus as the Son of the living God, toward the end of Jesus's earthly ministry Peter discovered that he was not yet walking in the character and humility of Christ. He was building his life and ministry with past victories and pride. Paul admonished us to take heed how we build on our foundation in Christ:

According to the grace of God which was given to me, as a wise master builder I have laid the foundation, and another builds on it. But let each one take heed how he builds on it. For no other foundation can anyone lay than that which is laid, which is Jesus Christ.
—1 CORINTHIANS 3:10–11

When any part of our lives is built upon worldly things, that part will be shaken by Christ.

Read 1 John 2:15–17. Below is a list of worldly things that God will shake from our lives. Put an x on the line representing where you are.

The lust of the flesh

_____

ALREADY SHAKEN   NEEDS TO BE SHAKEN

The lust of the eyes

_____

ALREADY SHAKEN   NEEDS TO BE SHAKEN

The pride of life

_____

ALREADY SHAKEN   NEEDS TO BE SHAKEN

Because of Peter's pride at the end of Jesus's ministry, Jesus told him, "Simon, Simon! Indeed, Satan has asked for you, that he may sift you as wheat" (Luke 22:31).

Jesus did not pray that Simon Peter would escape the intense shaking—He prayed that Peter's faith would not fail in the process.

Pride opened the door for the enemy to come in and sift Simon Peter. Now if Jesus had had the mentality of many within the church, He might have said, "Let's pray, guys, and bind this attack of the devil. We are not going to let Satan do this to our beloved Simon!" But look at what He said: "I have prayed for you, that your faith should not fail; and when you have returned to Me, strengthen your brethren" (Luke 22:32).

Jesus did not pray that Simon Peter would escape the intense shaking—He prayed that Peter's faith would not fail in the process. Jesus knew that out of this trial would emerge a new character, the one Simon Peter needed to fulfill his destiny and strengthen his brethren.

Satan had requested permission to shake Simon Peter so severely that he would lose his faith. The enemy's intent was to destroy this man of great potential who had received so much revelation. But God had a different purpose for the shaking, and, as always, God is way ahead of the devil.

God may shake our lives for one of the following purposes. If He is shaking your life, which of these reasons could be His purpose for you? (Check ✔ all that apply.)

❏ To bring your life closer to its foundation
❏ To remove what is dead, such as pride, from your life
❏ To harvest what is ripe within you
❏ To awaken a dormant area of your spiritual life
❏ To solidify your life so that the truth in your spirit man can
    no longer be separated from your soul and body

Any thought process or heart attitude that is rooted in selfishness or pride will be shaken and purged.

WRITE A PRAYER...

Asking the Lord to sift the pride, selfishness, and lust from your life.

_____

_____

_____

DAY 16

GRACE IS GIVEN
TO THE HUMBLE

Be clothed with humility, for "God resists the
proud, but gives grace to the humble."
—1 PETER 5:5

[Read the remainder of chapter 8, beginning with the heading "Grace
Is Given to the Humble."]

TRIALS IN THIS LIFE WILL EXPOSE WHAT IS IN YOUR HEART—
whether the offense is toward God or others. Tests either make
you bitter toward God and your peers, or they make you stronger. If you
pass the test of humility, your roots will shoot down deeper, stabilizing
you and your future. If you fail, you become offended, which can lead
to defilement with bitterness.

Simon Peter was shaken to the point that he could no longer
boast of being great. He had lost his natural confidence. He saw all
too clearly the futility of his own strong will. He had been humbled.
He was now a perfect candidate for the grace of God. God gives His
grace to the humble. Humility is a prerequisite.

Have you ever said to Christ, "Lord, I've served You and laid many
things down to follow You, so why is this difficult or terrible thing happening to me now?"

Tests either make you bitter toward God and your peers, or they make you stronger.

Christians who experience hurts and disappointments often become offended with the Lord because they believe He should give them special considerations for all that they have done for Him.

They are serving Him for the wrong reasons. We should not serve the Lord for *what He can do,* but rather for *who He is* and *what He has already done* for us. Those who become offended do not fully realize how great a debt He has already paid for their freedom. They have forgotten from what manner of death they were delivered. They see through natural eyes rather than eternal.

Are you serving the Lord out of pride, self-confidence, or the hope that He will reward you for your service with material things or an easy life?

Complete the following sentences:

My motivation for serving Christ is _____

_____.

My confidence rests in _____

_____.

The reward I expect from Him is _____

_____.

We can do nothing of eternal value in our own ability.

WRITE A PRAYER...

Asking the Lord to purify your heart and to take away all confidence in your flesh.

_____

_____

_____

DAY 17

THE ROCK OF OFFENSE

*"Behold, I lay in Zion a chief cornerstone, elect, precious,
and he who believes on Him will by no means be put to
shame." Therefore, to you who believe, He is precious; but
to those who are disobedient, "The stone which the builders
rejected has become the chief cornerstone," and "a stone
of stumbling and a rock of offense." They stumble, being
disobedient to the word, to which they also were appointed.*
—I PETER 2:6–8

[Read chapter 9.]

TODAY THE MEANING OF THE WORD *BELIEVE* HAS BEEN WEAK-
ened. In the eyes of most it has become a mere acknowledgment
of a certain fact. To many it has nothing to do with obedience. But in
the passage above, the words *believe* and *disobedient* are represented as
opposites.

The Scriptures exhort "that whoever believes in Him [Jesus
Christ] should not perish but have everlasting life" (John 3:16).

As a result of the way we view the word *believe,* many think
that all they are required to do is believe that Jesus existed and
died on Calvary to be in good standing with God. If this were the
only requirement, the demons would be in good standing with
Him, for the Scriptures also say, "You believe that there is one

God. You do well. Even the demons believe—and tremble!" (James 2:19). Yet, there is no salvation for them.

Complete these sentences:

For me, faith is _____

_____.

For me, obedience is _____

_____.

If I say I believe and do not obey, then _____

_____.

The word *believe* has more meaning in the Scriptures than that of merely acknowledging the existence of or mentally assenting to a fact. Remaining true to the context of the verse above, we can say that the main element of believing is obedience. We could read it this way: "Therefore, to you who obey, He is precious; but to those who are disobedient, 'The stone which the builders rejected has become the chief cornerstone,' and 'a stone of stumbling and a rock of offense.'"

Love is the bottom line in our relationship with the Lord—not love of principles or teachings, but love for the Person of Jesus Christ.

It is not difficult to obey when you know the character and love of the one to whom you are submitting. Love is the bottom line in our relationship with the Lord—not love of principles or teachings, but love for the Person of Jesus Christ. If that love is not firmly in place, we are susceptible to offense and to stumbling.

When you live in obedience to the will of God, you will not fulfill the desires of men. As a result, you will suffer in the flesh. Jesus suffered His greatest opposition from the religious leaders. Religious people believe God operates only within the confines of their parameters. If the Master offended religious people as He was led by the

Spirit two thousand years ago, those who follow Him today will surely offend them also.

Remember, your response determines your future. Complete this sentence:

When others are offended with me living for Christ, I will _____

_____.

Paul wrote: "The fact that the cross is the only way to salvation offends people, but that is the truth, and there's no way I'm going to preach anything else!" (See Galatians 5:11.)

If anyone challenges the truth of the gospel, it is time to be offensive without apology. We must determine in our hearts that we *will* obey the Spirit of God no matter the cost.

WRITE A PRAYER...

Telling Christ that you will trust, love, and obey Him.

_____

_____

_____

Day 18

LEST WE OFFEND THEM

Therefore let us not judge one another anymore,
but rather resolve this, not to put a stumbling
block or a cause to fall in our brother's way.
—ROMANS 14:13

[Read chapter 10, stopping at the heading "Laying Down Our Rights."]

THOUGH MANY PEOPLE WERE OFFENDED AT JESUS, HE NEVER caused an offense by asserting His personal rights or benefits. Jesus urged, "Therefore whoever humbles himself as this little child is the greatest in the kingdom of heaven" (Matt. 18:4). The key phrase here is "whoever humbles himself." A little later Jesus amplified this:

> Whoever desires to become great among you, let him be your servant. And whoever desires to be first among you, let him be your slave—just as the Son of Man did not come to be served, but to serve, and to give His life a ransom for many.
>
> —MATTHEW 20:26–28

What a statement! Jesus did not come to be served but to serve. He was the Son of God. He was free. He owed no one anything. He was subject to no man. Yet He chose to use His liberty and freedom to serve.

Jesus chose to use His liberty and freedom to serve.

Read the following passages, and jot down what each Scripture teaches about serving and being a servant.

Luke 16:13

_____

_____

Luke 22:26

_____

_____

John 12:26

_____

_____

Romans 7:6

_____

_____

Galatians 5:13

_____

_____

Philippians 2:5–11

_____

_____

Notice that Paul emphasizes in Galatians 5:13 that we have been given the privilege or the opportunity to serve one another. We are not to use our liberty or privileges as children of the living God to serve ourselves. Liberty is to be used to serve others. There is freedom in serving but bondage in slavery. A slave is one who has to serve, while a servant is one who lives to serve.

I have seen many Christians serve with a resentful attitude. They give grudgingly and complain as they pay their taxes. They still live as slaves to a law from which they have been set free. They remain slaves in their hearts.

WRITE A PRAYER...

Renouncing slavery to the world and surrendering yourself to be Christ's servant.

_____

_____

_____

_____

DAY 19

LAYING DOWN OUR RIGHTS

But beware lest somehow this liberty of yours become
a stumbling block to those who are weak.
—1 CORINTHIANS 8:9

[Read the remainder of chapter 10, beginning with the heading
"Laying Down Our Rights."]

OUR LIBERTY HAS BEEN GIVEN TO US FOR SERVING AND LAYING down our lives. We are to build and not destroy, to edify and not tear down. This liberty was not given to enable us to heap gain upon ourselves. Because we have used it in this manner, many today are offended by the lifestyles of Christians. We may have the freedom in Christ to do many things, but if something will offend another person, then we must carefully consider voluntarily limiting ourselves in order to witness to others.

Do the things I do seek the edification of another or myself?

Make a list of things that you have voluntarily stopped doing so that you will not offend or be a stumbling block to others.

I have given up the right to: So as not to offend:

_____   _____

_____   _____

_____   _____

_____   _____

_____   _____

How do we know what freedoms and rights we need to set aside in order to win others to Christ? I suggest applying what I call the "edification test."

The apostle Paul, in writing to the Romans, summed up the heart of God in the matter: "Therefore let us pursue the things which make for peace and the things by which one may edify another" (Rom. 14:19).

What we do may even be permissible according to the Scriptures. But ask yourself: Does it seek the edification of another or myself?

Read the following passage slowly. Underline every part that is hard for you to do. Circle the part that you need to start doing immediately.

> All things are lawful for me, but not all things are helpful; all things are lawful for me, but not all things edify. Let no one seek his own, but each one the other's well-being....Therefore, whether you eat or drink, or whatever you do, do all to the glory of God. Give no offense, either to the Jews or to the Greeks or to the church of God, just as I also please all men in all things, not seeking my own profit, but the profit of many, that they may be saved.
>
> —1 CORINTHIANS 10:23–24, 31–33

Allow the Holy Spirit to funnel every area of your life through this Scripture passage. Allow Him to show you any hidden motives or agendas that are for your profit and not for the profit of others. No matter what area of life you might embrace, accept His challenge to live as a servant of all.

WRITE A PRAYER...

Asking the Lord to show you anything in your life that may be a stumbling block to others, and then remove it.

_____

_____

_____

_____

Day 20

FORGIVENESS: YOU DON'T GIVE—YOU DON'T GET

Therefore I say to you, whatever things you ask when you pray, believe that you receive them, and you will have them. And whenever you stand praying, if you have anything against anyone, forgive him, that your Father in heaven may also forgive you your trespasses. But if you do not forgive, neither will your Father in heaven forgive your trespasses.
—Mark 11:24–26

[Read chapter 11, stopping at the heading "The Unforgiving Servant."]

Let's turn our attention to the consequences of refusing to let go of offense and how to get free from offense. Jesus meant what He said: "But if you do not forgive, neither will your Father in heaven forgive your trespasses."

We live in a culture where we don't always mean what we say. Consequently we do not believe others mean what they say to us. A person's word is not taken seriously.

It begins in childhood. A parent tells a child, "If you do that again, you'll get a spanking." The child not only does it again but several times more after that. Following each episode the child receives the same warning from his parent. Usually no corrective action is taken. If correction does take place, it is either lighter than what was promised or more severe because the parent is frustrated.

Are you forgiving others so that you might receive forgiveness?

But when Jesus speaks, He wants us to take Him seriously. We cannot view what He says the way we view the other authorities or relations in our lives. When He says something, He means it. He is faithful even when we are faithless. He walks at a level of truth and integrity that transcends our culture or society. So when Jesus said, "But if you do not forgive, neither will your Father in heaven forgive your trespasses," He meant it.

Jot down what Jesus had to say about forgiveness in the Gospels.

Matthew 6:14–15

_____

_____

_____

Luke 6:37

_____

_____

_____

Matthew 6:12

_____

_____

_____

Are you taking Jesus seriously? Are you forgiving others so that you might receive forgiveness? When your heart is filled with unforgiveness, then there is no room in it to receive God's forgiveness.

WRITE A PRAYER...

Asking God to enable you to truly forgive the people who have offended you so that you will be able to receive God's forgiveness.

DAY 21

THE UNFORGIVING SERVANT

*Then Peter came to Him and said, "Lord, how often
shall my brother sin against me, and I forgive him? Up
to seven times?" Jesus said to him, "I do not say to you,
up to seven times, but up to seventy times seven."*
—MATTHEW 18:21–22

*[Read the remainder of chapter 11, beginning with the heading "The
Unforgiving Servant."]*

JESUS TAUGHT PETER AND THE DISCIPLES THAT FORGIVING OTHERS
is based on God's unlimited forgiveness. To emphasize this, Jesus
told the parable of the unforgiving servant.

*Read again this parable in Matthew 18:23–35. Then complete these
sentences:*

For me, the main point of the parable is _____

_____.

What I hear God saying to me through this parable is _____

_____.

The offenses we hold against each other, compared to our offenses against God, are like $4,000 compared to $14.5 billion. We may have been treated badly by someone else, but it does not compare with our transgressions against God. When we realize that Jesus delivered us from eternal death and torment, we will release others unconditionally.

Rank the following offenses that are the most difficult (1) to the least difficult (7) for you to forgive.

_____ Gossip against me

_____ Someone physically or emotionally abusing me

_____ Someone physically or emotionally abusing someone I love

_____ Someone lying to me

_____ Someone stealing from me

_____ Someone manipulating me

_____ Other _____

WRITE A PRAYER...

Asking God to remove the blockage in your heart that has been caused by unforgiveness. Pray specifically for the individuals whose offenses caused the blockage.

_____

_____

_____

DAY 22

REVENGE: THE TRAP

*Repay no one evil for evil. Have regard for
good things in the sight of all men.*
—ROMANS 12:17

[Read chapter 12, stopping at the heading "A Potential King Defiled."]

HOLDING ON TO AN OFFENSE OF UNFORGIVENESS IS LIKE HOLDING a debt against someone. When one person is wronged by another, he believes a debt is owed him. He expects payment of some sort, whether monetary or not. However, it is unrighteous for us as children of God to avenge ourselves.

Read the following scriptures, and then, in a phrase, summarize what they teach about revenge.

Romans 12:19

_____

_____

James 4:12; 5:9

_____

_____

Matthew 5:38–42

_____

_____

Jesus eliminates any gray areas for grudges. In fact, He says that our attitude is to be so far removed from avenging ourselves that we are willing to open ourselves to the possibility of being taken advantage of again.

> **We are admonished to be rooted and grounded in the love of God.**

Jesus likened the condition of our hearts to that of soil. We are admonished to be rooted and grounded in the love of God. The seed of God's Word will then take root in our hearts, will grow, and will eventually produce the fruit of righteousness—love, joy, long-suffering, peace, kindness, goodness, faithfulness, gentleness, and self-control. (See Galatians 5:22–23.)

However, ground will produce only what is planted in it. If we plant seeds of debt, unforgiveness, and offense, another root will spring up in place of the love of God. It is called the root of bitterness (Heb. 12:14–15). Bitterness is a root. If roots are nursed, watered, protected, fed, and given attention, they increase in depth and strength. If not dealt with quickly, roots are hard to pull up. The strength of the offense will continue to grow. Soon, instead of the fruit of righteousness being produced, we will see a harvest of anger, resentment, jealousy, hatred, strife, and discord. Jesus called these evil fruits worthless. (See Matthew 7:19–20.)

WRITE A PRAYER...

Thanking God that His peace has come into your life as a result of releasing the offenses that had blocked your heart.

_____

_____

_____

DAY 23

A POTENTIAL KING DEFILED

And Absalom spoke to his brother Amnon neither
good nor bad. For Absalom hated Amnon,
because he had forced his sister Tamar.
—2 SAMUEL 13:22

[Read the remainder of chapter 12, beginning with the heading "A
Potential King Defiled."]

ABSALOM AVENGED TAMAR'S RAPE BY MURDERING AMNON. HE
also held bitterness in his heart against David for not punishing
Amnon for the rape of Absalom's sister. Absalom's thoughts were poisoned with bitterness. He became an expert critic of David's weaknesses. Yet he hoped his father would call for him. When David did not, this fueled Absalom's resentment.

Out of this offended critical attitude, Absalom began to draw to himself anyone who was discontented. He made himself available to all Israel, taking time to listen to their complaints. He lamented that things would be different if only he were king. He judged their cases, since it appeared the king had no time for them. Perhaps Absalom judged their cases because he felt he had not been served justice in his own.

He seemed to be concerned for the people. The Bible says Absalom stole the hearts of Israel from his father, David. But was he genuinely concerned for them, or was he seeking a way to overthrow David, the one who had offended him?

The Holy Spirit convicts as He speaks through one's conscience.

Assistants to leaders in a church often become offended by the person they serve. They soon become critical, experts at all that is wrong with their leader, or those he or she appoints. They become offended. Their sight is distorted. They see from a totally different perspective than God's.

Complete the following sentences:

When people come to me with criticisms of church leadership, I _____

_____

_____.

When I am critical of church leadership, I _____

_____

_____.

The most effective way to handle offenses in the body of Christ is

_____

_____.

Make a list of any people in the church who offend you, including the leadership. Write down their names, and then write down the date when you will go to them and ask forgiveness for your offense.

Name   When you will ask forgiveness

_____   _____

_____   _____

_____   _____

_____   _____

_____   _____

Sometimes your observations about the weaknesses of church leadership are correct. Perhaps David should have taken action against Amnon. Perhaps a leader has areas of error. But who is the judge—you or the Lord? Remember that if you sow strife, you will reap it.

The Holy Spirit convicts as He speaks through one's conscience. We must not ignore His conviction or quench His voice. If you have done this, repent before God and open your heart to His correction.

WRITE A PRAYER...

Asking God to remove a critical spirit from you.

_____

_____

_____

DAY 24

ESCAPING THE TRAP

*This being so, I myself always strive to have a
conscience without offense toward God and men.*
—ACTS 24:16

[Read chapter 13, stopping at the heading "Healing in Confrontation."]

IT TAKES EFFORT TO STAY FREE FROM OFFENSE. PAUL COMPARES IT
to exercising. If we exercise our bodies, we are less prone to injury.
When we exercise forgiveness and refuse to take up offenses, then we
keep our consciences fit and clean.

It takes effort to stay free from offense.

Sometimes others offend us, and it is not hard to forgive. We have
exercised our hearts so they are in condition to handle offense; therefore, no injury or permanent damage results. But some offenses will be
more challenging than those for which we've been trained to handle.
This extra strain may cause a wound or injury, after which we will
have to exercise spiritually to be healed again. But the result will be
worth the effort. Are you facing a hurtful, serious wound? The exercise
needed for recovery is listed below.

*After reading each step, write down the specific response you will make
in order to achieve recovery.*

1. *Recognize that you are hurt.*

   I have been hurt by _____

   _____.

2. *Confess your hurt to the Lord.*

   Lord, I confess that I was hurt when _____

   _____.

3. *Be open to His correction and direction.*

   Lord, I understand that You desire me to _____

   _____.

4. *Finally, we must forgive the person(s) who hurt us.*

   Jesus, I forgive _____

   for _____.

The next exercise we face after we have forgiven someone is to avoid relapsing. Occasionally, we may find ourselves having to fight off some of the same thoughts we had about that person before we forgave him or her. The way we do this is to remember to pray for that person. These scriptures will help you know how to pray.

Read each scripture, and jot down the attitude God desires us to have in our hearts for those who hurt us.

Matthew 5:44

_____

_____

Psalm 35:11–14

_____

_____

2 Corinthians 10:5

_____

_____

WRITE A PRAYER...

Praying for the deepest needs of someone who has hurt you.

_____

_____

_____

DAY 25

HEALING IN CONFRONTATION

*And above all things have fervent love for one
another, for "love will cover a multitude of sins."*
—I PETER 4:8

*[Read the remainder of chapter 13, beginning with the heading
"Healing in Confrontation."]*

THERE ARE TIMES WHEN THE ONLY PATH TO HEALING LEADS
through confrontation. It is easy to love those who can do no wrong
in our eyes—that's honeymoon love. It is another thing to love someone
when we can see their faults, especially when we've been their victims.

Hard places and difficult challenges will always be a part of our
journey with the Lord. We cannot escape them. We need to face
them, for they are part of the process of being perfected in Him. If
you choose to run from them, you will seriously hinder your growth.

As you overcome different obstacles, you will be stronger
and more compassionate. You will fall more in love with Jesus. If
you have come out of hardships and do not feel this way, you have
probably not recovered from the offense. You must make the choice to
recover. Some people get hurt and never recover because they have not
chosen to do so.

❏ If you are still hurting from a past offense, it is because you choose to hurt.

❏ The only way to be healed is to forgive. Release the offense and offending person to God.

❏ A lack of compassion for others arises from an unwillingness to forgive their weaknesses.

❏ Your spiritual maturity depends on your willingness to face, forgive, and forget past offenses.

Jesus learned obedience by the things He suffered. Peter learned obedience by the things he suffered. Paul learned obedience by the things he suffered.

Your spiritual maturity depends on your willingness to face, forgive, and forget past offenses.

What about you? Have you learned? As a result of past offenses, how are you now feeling?

In each of the columns below, check ✔ *the appropriate boxes to indicate your feelings right now.*

HEALED FEELINGS	HURT FEELINGS
❏ Free	❏ Burdened
❏ Forgiving	❏ Unforgiving
❏ Loving	❏ Vengeful
❏ Gentle	❏ Calloused
❏ Compassionate	❏ Judgmental
❏ Accepting	❏ Rejecting
❏ Humble	❏ Proud
❏ Warmhearted	❏ Coldhearted
❏ Peaceful	❏ Angry
❏ Joyful	❏ Depressed
❏ Healed	❏ Broken
❏ Refreshed	❏ Bitter

If you find yourself checking more hurt feelings than healed feelings, then the process of your healing has stopped; you will not obey God's leading and mature spiritually.

Maturity does not come easily. If it did, all would attain it. Few reach this level of life because of the resistance they face. The world is dominated by the "prince of the power of the air" (Eph. 2:2). The course of our society is not godly but selfish. As a result, to enter into the maturity of Christ there will be hardships that come from standing against the flow of selfishness.

Remember that when we lose our life for the sake of Jesus, we will find His life. Learn to fix your focus on the end result, not the struggle. (See 1 Peter 4:12–13.)

WRITE A PRAYER...

Thanking God for the trials and tribulations you have faced. Thank Him for the results that have come as a result of these struggles.

_____

_____

_____

DAY 26

OBJECTIVE: RECONCILIATION

*You have heard that it was said to those of old, "You
shall not murder, and whoever murders will be in
danger of the judgment." But I say to you that whoever
is angry with his brother without a cause shall be
in danger of the judgment.... First be reconciled to
your brother, and then come and offer your gift.*
—MATTHEW 5:21–22, 24

*[Read chapter 14, stopping at the heading "Asking Forgiveness of One
Who Is Offended."]*

IN THE SERMON ON THE MOUNT, JESUS FIRST QUOTES THE LAW
regulating our outward actions. Then He shows its fulfillment by
bringing it into the heart. (See Matthew 5:21–22, 24.) In God's eyes a
murderer is not limited to one who commits murder—he is also the one
who hates his brother. What you are in your heart is who you really are!

Jesus clearly delineates the consequences of offense in this portion of His sermon. He illustrates the severity of holding anger or
bitter offense. If one is angry with his brother without a cause, he is
in danger of judgment. Jesus was showing them that not dealing with
anger can lead to hatred. Hatred not dealt with would put them in
danger of hell. Jesus admonished His followers to seek reconciliation
as a top priority in response to offense.

We seek to be reconciled with such urgency, not for our own sakes alone, but for our brother's sake. We can become a catalyst to help him out of the offense. The love of God does not permit us to allow him to remain angry without attempting to reach out to him in restoration. We may have done nothing wrong. Right or wrong doesn't matter. It is more important for us to help this stumbling brother than to prove ourselves correct.

Often we judge ourselves by our *intentions* and judge everyone else by their *actions*.

Make a list of any persons with whom you have an offense. By each name write down the time and date when you will go to that person, seeking to be reconciled.

Name	Date	Time

Often we judge ourselves by our *intentions* and judge everyone else by their *actions*. It is possible to intend one thing while communicating something totally different. Sometimes our true motives are cleverly hidden, even from us. We want to believe they are pure. But as we filter them through the Word of God we see them differently. If you need to be reconciled, good motives are not enough. It's time to go immediately and be reconciled. Will you go?

WRITE A PRAYER...

Asking God to empower you with love and boldness to go and be reconciled to anyone with whom you have experienced offense.

_____

_____

_____

Day 27

ASKING FORGIVENESS OF
ONE WHO IS OFFENDED

*Therefore let us pursue the things which make for peace
and the things by which one may edify another.*
—Romans 14:19

[Read the section in chapter 14 titled "Asking Forgiveness of One Who Is Offended."]

Romans 14:19 shows us how to approach a person we have offended. If we go with an attitude of frustration, we will not promote peace. We will only make it difficult for the one who is hurt. We should pursue peace through humility at the expense of our pride. It is the only way to see true reconciliation.

On certain occasions I have approached people I have hurt or who were angry with me, and they have lashed out at me. I have been told I was selfish, inconsiderate, proud, rude, harsh, and more.

My natural response has been to say, "No, I'm not. You just don't understand me!" But when I defend myself, it only fuels their fire of offense. This is not pursuing peace. Standing up for ourselves and "our rights" will never bring true peace.

Instead I have learned to listen and keep my mouth shut until they have said what they need to say. If I don't agree, I let them know

I respect what they have said and will search my attitude and intentions. Then I tell them I am sorry I have hurt them.

Godly wisdom is having a willingness to yield.

Other times they are accurate in their assessment of me, and I admit, "You are right. I ask your forgiveness."

Recall a recent time when you asked someone to forgive you. Briefly indicate the approach you used with them. Circle anything prideful that you said or did.

_____

_____

_____

Humbling ourselves will promote reconciliation. Pride defends, but humility agrees and says, "You are right. I have acted this way. Please forgive me."

Read James 3:17 and rewrite it in your own words.

_____

_____

_____

Godly wisdom is having a willingness to yield. Godly wisdom is not stiff-necked or stubborn when it comes to personal conflicts. A person submitted to godly wisdom is not afraid to yield or defer to the other person's viewpoint as long as it does not violate truth.

WRITE A PRAYER...

Asking God to reveal offenses in your heart and to give you wisdom to approach those you have offended.

_____

_____

DAY 28

APPROACHING SOMEONE
WHO HAS OFFENDED YOU

Moreover if your brother sins against you, go and
tell him his fault between you and him alone. If
he hears you, you have gained your brother.
—MATTHEW 18:15

[Read the section in chapter 14 titled "Approaching Someone Who Has Offended You."]

MANY PEOPLE APPLY MATTHEW 18:15 IN A DIFFERENT SPIRIT than the one Jesus intended. If hurt, they confront the offender in a spirit of revenge and anger, using the verse to justify their condemnation of the one who has hurt them. But they have misunderstood the reason Jesus instructed us to go to one another. It is not for *condemnation* but for *reconciliation*. Jesus does not want us to tell our brother how rotten he has been to us. We are to repair the breach that prevents the restoration of our relationship.

This is the way God uses to restore us to Himself. Though we have sinned against God, He "demonstrates His own love toward [and for] us, in that while we were still sinners, Christ died for us" (Rom. 5:8). Are we willing to lay down our self-protection and die to pride in order to be restored to the one who has offended us? God reached out to us before we asked for forgiveness. Jesus decided to forgive us before we even acknowledged our offense.

Carefully read Romans 5:6–11, and then respond to the following statements:

My condition when God reached out to me was _____

_____.

God's reaching out to me demonstrated _____

_____.

The reason He reached out to me was _____

_____.

What God accomplished in reaching out to me was _____

_____.

Even though He reached out to us, we could not be reconciled to the Father until we received His word of reconciliation.

We are to repair the breach that prevents the restoration of our relationship.

In the New Testament, the disciples preached that the people had sinned against God. But why tell people they have sinned? To condemn them? God does not condemn. "For God did not send His Son into the world to condemn the world, but that the world through Him might be saved" (John 3:17). Rather it is to bring them to a place where they realize their condition, repent of their sins, and ask forgiveness.

WRITE A PRAYER...

Repenting and asking God to help you reconcile with anyone you have offended or who has offended you.

_____

_____

_____

DAY 29

THE BOTTOM LINE

*If it is possible, as much as depends on
you, live peaceably with all men.*
—ROMANS 12:18

[Read the section in chapter 14 titled "The Bottom Line."]

IF WE KEEP THE LOVE OF GOD AS OUR MOTIVATION, WE WILL NOT
fail. Love never fails. When we love others the way Jesus loves us, we
will be free even if the other person chooses not to be reconciled to us.

Jesus says, "If it is possible," because there are times when others
will refuse to be at peace with us. Or there may be those who demand
conditions for reconciliation that would compromise our relationship with the Lord. In either case, it is not possible to restore that
relationship.

God says, "…as much as depends on you." We are to do everything we can to be reconciled with another person as long as we
remain loyal to truth. We often give up on relationships too soon.

Jesus said, "Blessed are the *peacemakers*, for they shall be called
sons of God" (Matt. 5:9, emphasis added). He did not say, "Blessed
are the *peacekeepers*." A peacekeeper avoids confrontation at all costs
to maintain peace, even at the risk of compromising truth. The peace
he maintains is not true peace. It is a touchy, superficial peace that will
not last.

Love never fails, never fades, and never comes to an end.

A peacemaker will confront in love, bringing truth so that the resulting reconciliation will endure. He will not maintain an artificial, superficial relationship. He desires openness, truth, and love. He refuses to hide offense with a political smile. He makes peace with a bold love that cannot fail.

How effective a peacemaker are you? Below are some qualities of peacemakers. Put yourself on the line with an x.

Peacemakers are…

Loving		*Quick to listen*	
❑ I am	❑ I need to be	❑ I am	❑ I need to be
Patient		*Slow to anger*	
❑ I am	❑ I need to be	❑ I am	❑ I need to be
Forgiving		*Slow to speak*	
❑ I am	❑ I need to be	❑ I am	❑ I need to be
Open		*Obedient*	
❑ I am	❑ I need to be	❑ I am	❑ I need to be
Vulnerable		*Hearing God*	
❑ I am	❑ I need to be	❑ I am	❑ I need to be
Truthful		*Humble*	
❑ I am	❑ I need to be	❑ I am	❑ I need to be

Jesus demonstrated all these qualities. When the Spirit of the Prince of Peace indwells us, we have the power to be all of these things. He is not willing that any should perish. But He will not compromise truth for a relationship. He seeks reconciliation with true commitment, not on superficial terms. This develops a bond of love that no evil can sever. He has laid down His life for us. We can only do likewise.

Love never fails, never fades, and never comes to an end. It seeks not its own. It is not easily offended. (See 1 Corinthians 13.)

WRITE A PRAYER...

Asking God to fill you with His love for others—especially for your enemies and for those who could offend you.

_____

_____

_____

Day 30

TAKING ACTION

Therefore, to him who knows to do good
and does not do it, to him it is sin.
—James 4:17

[Read the epilogue, "Taking Action."]

Now is the time to act! Ask the Lord to remind you of offenses you have hidden, forgotten, or denied. Ask the Holy Spirit to walk you through your past, bringing to mind the people with whom you have an offense.

When you know that your heart has been cleansed of past offenses and is strong and settled, stand firm and resist Satan's bait in the future.

Be ready to pray and ask forgiveness. Prepare to go to them in humility to ask forgiveness and to be reconciled. Use the prayer in the epilogue as a guideline for your prayer.

As you prepare to pray, jot down your responses to the following statements:

During this thirty-day devotional program, the most important thing I have learned is _____

_____

_____.

When tempted by the bait of Satan, I will _____

_____

_____.

The next step I need to take personally in order to resist offense with people is _____

_____

_____.

One person I need to immediately ask for forgiveness is _____

_____

_____.

One reason I need to keep a spiritual journal is _____

_____

_____.

In regard to offenses, I need to pray daily that _____

_____

_____.

When you know that your heart has been cleansed of past offenses and is strong and settled, stand firm and resist Satan's bait in the future. Read about the whole armor of God in Ephesians 6:10–18. You will be an overcomer and will defeat the enemy!

WRITE A PRAYER...

Thanking God for the specific protection He gives with each piece of spiritual armor He has provided for you.

_____

_____

_____

Extraordinary
CURRICULUM

The *Extraordinary* Curriculum is an extensive journey with 12 video and audio sessions, a thought-provoking devotional workbook, and a hardcover book. As each session builds, you will be positioned to step into the unknown and embrace your divine empowerment.

INCLUDES:
- 12 30-MINUTE VIDEO SESSIONS ON 4 DVDs
- 12 30-MINUTE AUDIO SESSIONS ON 6 CDs
- HARDCOVER BOOK
- DEVOTIONAL WORKBOOK
- PROMOTIONAL MATERIALS

BREAKING INTIMIDATION
CURRICULUM

Everyone has been intimidated at some point in life. Do you really know why it happened or how to keep it from happening again? John Bevere exposes the root of intimidation, challenges you to break its fearful grip, and teaches you to release God's gifts and establish His dominion in your life.

INCLUDES:
- EIGHT 30-MINUTE VIDEO SESSIONS ON 3 DVDs
- EIGHT 30-MINUTE AUDIO SESSIONS ON 4 CDs
- BREAKING INTIMIDATION BOOK
- DEVOTIONAL WORKBOOK
- PROMOTIONAL MATERIALS

INCLUDES:
- 12 30-MINUTE VIDEO LESSONS ON 4 DVDs
- 12 30-MINUTE AUDIO LESSONS ON 6 CDs
- HONOR'S REWARD HARDCOVER BOOK
- DEVOTIONAL WORKBOOK
- PROMOTIONAL MATERIALS

HONOR'S REWARD
CURRICULUM

This curriculum will unveil the power and truth of an often overlooked principle–Honor. If you understand the vital role of this virtue, you will attract blessing both now and for eternity. This insightful message teaches you how to extend honor to your Creator, family members, authorities and those who surround your world.

DRIVEN *by* Eternity
CURRICULUM

Making Your Life Count Today & Forever

We were made for eternity. This life on earth is but a vapor. Yet too many live as though there is nothing on the other side. Scriptural laws and principles may be applied to achieve success on earth, but are we prepared for eternity? This power-packed teaching, including an allegory on the Kingdom of Affabel, will help you understand that the choices you make today will determine how you spend eternity.

INCLUDES:
- 12 40-MINUTE VIDEO LESSONS ON 4 DVDs
- DRIVEN BY ETERNITY HARDCOVER BOOK
- HARDCOVER DEVOTIONAL WORKBOOK
- AFFABEL AUDIO THEATER

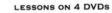

RESCUED

2 hours on 2 CDs **AUDIO THEATER**

From the novel *Rescued*

Starring:
    Roma Downey from *Touched by an Angel*
    John Rhys-Davies from *The Lord of the Rings*
    Marisol Nichols from the hit TV show *24*

A trapped father. A desperate son. A clock ticking down toward certain death and a fate even more horrible still...

For Alan Rockaway, his teenaged son Jeff, and his new bride Jenny, it's been little more than a leisurely end to a weeklong cruise...

a horrifying crash and even more, a plunge toward the unknown...Everything Alan has assumed about himself is flipped upside down. In the ultimate rescue operation, life or death is just the beginning!

AFFABEL
WINDOW of ETERNITY

2.5 hours on 4 CDs

FEATURING JOHN RHYS-DAVIES AND A CAST OF HOLLYWOOD ACTORS

AN EPIC AUDIO THEATER PORTRAYING THE REALITY OF THE JUDGMENT SEAT OF CHRIST. GET READY TO BE CHANGED FOREVER...AND PREPARE FOR ETERNITY!

This audio dramatization, taken from John Bevere's book, *Driven by Eternity*, will capture your heart and soul as you experience life on "the other side" where eternity is brought into the present and all must stand before the Great King and Judge. Be prepared for a roller coaster ride of joy, sorrow, astonishment, and revelation as lifelong rewards are bestowed on some while others are bound hand and foot and cast into outer darkness by the Royal Guard!

BOOKS BY JOHN

The Bait of Satan
Breaking Intimidation
Drawing Near
Driven by Eternity
Enemy Access Denied
Extraordinary
The Fear of the Lord
A Heart Ablaze

Honor's Reward
How to Respond When You Feel Mistreated
Rescued
Thus Saith the Lord
Under Cover
Victory in the Wilderness
The Voice of One Crying

life-transforming truth.

Messenger International.

Messenger International, founded by John and Lisa Bevere, imparts the fear of the Lord while inspiring freedom through the spoken and written Word to release people into their fulfilled lives in Christ.

UNITED STATES
P.O. Box 888
Palmer Lake, CO
80133-0888
800-648-1477 (US & Canada)
Tel: 719-487-3000
mail@MessengerInternational.org

AUSTRALIA
Rouse Hill Town Centre
P.O. Box 6444
Rouse Hill NSW 2155
In AUS: 1-300-650-577
Tel: +61 2 9679 4900
aus@MessengerInternational.org

EUROPE
P.O. Box 1066
Hemel, Hempstead HP2 7GQ
United Kingdom
In UK: 0800 9808 933
Tel: +44 1442 288 531
europe@MessengerInternational.org

The Messenger television program broadcasts in over 200 countries including the U.S. on GOD TV, the Australian Christian Channel and the New Life Channel in Russia.
Please check your local listings for day and time.

www.MessengerInternational.org

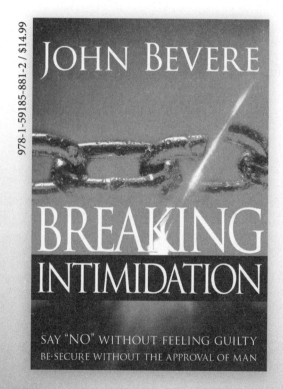